Maxwell Museum of Anthropology
Publication Series

GENERAL EDITORS

J. J. Brody
Mari Lyn Salvador

TIJERAS CANYON

THIS BOOK ACCOMPANIES THE EXHIBITION TIJERAS CANYON: ANALYSES OF THE PAST, WHICH OPENED ON OCTOBER 5, 1980, AT THE MAXWELL MUSEUM OF ANTHROPOLOGY.

TIJERAS CANYON

Analyses of the Past

Edited by
Linda S. Cordell

Published by
The Maxwell Museum of Anthropology
and
The University of New Mexico Press
Albuquerque

Library of Congress Cataloging in Publication Data
Main entry under title:

Tijeras Canyon: analyses of the past.

   (Maxwell Museum of Anthropology publication series)
   Bibliography: p. 187
   Includes index.
   1. Indians of North America—New Mexico—Tijeras
Canyon—Antiquities.   2. Pueblo Indians—Antiquities.
3. Tijeras Canyon, N.M.—Antiquities.   4. New Mexico—
Antiquities.   I. Cordell Linda S.   II. Series: Maxwell
Museum of Anthropology. Maxwell Museum of Anthropology
publication series.
E78.N65T54   978.9′61   80-52275
ISBN 0-8263-0553-9

This publication has been financed in part with federal funds from the Heritage Conservation and Recreation Service, Department of the Interior, through the Historic Preservation
Bureau, State Planning Division, Department of Finance and Administration of the State of
New Mexico. However, the contents and opinions of this volume do not necessarily reflect
the views or policies of the Department of the Interior, nor does the mention of trade names
or commercial products constitute endorsement or recommendation by the Department of
the Interior.

Contents

List of Figures

List of Tables

Preface

This volume is concerned with recent archaeological research carried out in Tijeras Canyon, New Mexico by two institutions. Between 1971 and 1976, the University of New Mexico's summer field school in archaeology conducted an inventory survey of 25 sections in the Tijeras Canyon–South Sandia area and excavated about one third of Tijeras Pueblo (LA 581). (Numbers following site names refer to the site inventory maintained by the Museum of New Mexico's Laboratory of Anthropology). A portion of the field school survey was funded by a grant from the New Mexico State Planning Office (Judge 1974; Cordell 1975, 1977a, 1977b; Blevins and Joiner 1977). From 1972 to 1975, the Laboratory of Anthropology of the Museum of New Mexico conducted survey, excavation, and ethnohistorical research in the canyon in connection with the expansion of Interstate 40 and New Mexico Highway North 14 (Snow 1976; Farwell 1977; Oakes 1978; Swadesh 1976, 1977). Contributors to this volume represent both institutions.

Dana Anderson served as field supervisor for the Museum's excavation at Coconito (A 10794) and assistant supervisor at San Antonio (LA 23). Yvonne Oakes was the Museum's field supervisor of excavations at four small sites in the vicinity of Dead Man's Curve. Anderson and Oakes are currently graduate students in anthropology at the University of New Mexico, and their paper represents work done at the University. A. Helene Warren was geological consultant for the Museum's project. She is also a graduate student in anthropology at the University of New Mexico where her contribution to this volume was prepared. Frances Leon (Swadesh) Quintana and David Kayser pursued their ethnohistorical and archaeological studies as part of the Museum's work at San Antonio. Cheryl Ferguson, Emily Garber, and Gwen Young were students on the University's field school. Their work and Bennie Phillips's chapter derive from additional analyses of the field school materials that were undertaken while they served as research assistants in the Department of Anthropology at the University. I became director of the field school in 1974 and served in that capacity through 1976.

The field work in Tijeras Canyon generated considerable public interest. The proximity of excavations to major highways encouraged daily visits from Albuquerque residents and from tourists passing through. In addition, we had contacted many residents of the canyon in the course of our work and enjoyed their cooperation and their interest in our finds. Our field work was carried out in the summer when temperatures in the high 90°s (F.) were not uncommon. Despite the heat and dust that was at times nearly suffocating in the immediate vicinity of the excavations, visitors to the sites stood (or sat) for hours and watched the work progress. The excavation crews deployed "tour guides" to escort visitors around the excavations and to explain the techniques being used to unearth information from the sites (Figure 1). Our visitors asked many interesting questions such as, How were the sites dated? Why did we take flotation samples? Where was the pottery made? Why were the sites abandoned? Although we tried to answer questions as fully as possible, we realized that our visitors were only seeing about a third of our work. They did not have the opportunity to view and evaluate the analysis of archaeological materials as that phase of the investigation was carried out.

The questions of our summer visitors reminded me that public exposure to archaeology is apt to include only two points in the process of research. Thus, the public may often be welcome to see field work in process and to read the final interpretive summary of the prehistory of a site or a region. Archaeological research actually involves four phases that may overlap in time. First, background research is done to establish a research design or focus for a project. The design is used to direct the nature, scope, and techniques employed in field work. Second, field work is done. During the course of excavation or site survey, information is analyzed and adjustments to recovery techniques or strategies are made. When field work is complete, analysis continues, involving the work of specialists in various fields. For example, hundreds of wood specimens from Tijeras Pueblo were sent to the Tree-ring Laboratory at the University of Arizona for dating, hundreds of hours were spent examining faunal remains for butchering marks, and time was spent preparing slides and identifying plant seeds. None of this work generally is seen by interested visitors to the sites. The final phase of research is the preparation of a report. These are public documents, but most are written for professional archaeologists.

1. Young visitors on a tour of Tijeras Pueblo excavations. The tour guide is UNM field school student Stephen Lent.

Most books and articles available to the broader, general audience are based on interpretations of the results of analyses that the nonprofessional has never seen. Although the interpretations are usually sound, it requires a leap of faith for the interested person to watch an excavation in process and then believe that, for example, the site in question was abandoned because a local water supply failed in A.D. 1490. The analyses crucial to the interpretation, the sifting and weighing of evidence and the exploring of alternatives, make up the bulk of the scientific process and are rarely discussed. This book, which is about analysis, accepts the premise that the interest shown in archaeology by visitors to a site (who are willing to spend physically uncomfortable hours watching excavation) is high enough that the details of analysis are important to them as well. Even those who read only the regional syntheses eventually produced should be interested in understanding the methods of analysis on which these are based. This book provides an invitation to those who would like to know how we, as archaeologists and anthropologists, think we know what we know.

There is another, very personal, rationale for the form of this book. As a field school director, I am committed to providing training for students in all phases of professional research. During the field school's work at Tijeras Pueblo, students worked closely with staff members in excavation and in analysis. Dialogue among students and staff, at the site, in laboratories, at lectures and on field trips, was constant and mutually stimulating. All students contributed to the research process, and they were expected to know how their work fit in with overall scientific goals. A weekly "ritual" developed during the course of field work at Tijeras. This was the "Monday Morning Walk-around," a time when students explained to all participants on the dig how their work of the previous week added to our research (Figure 2). After the field work had been completed, students continued analysis of

2. Field school students during a typical Monday Morning Walk-around.

materials during the ensuing academic semesters. Their analyses provide the foundations for the local and regional syntheses of future prehistories. Their work also constitutes a critical part of their professional growth. I believe that professional training includes the obligation to share one's work with as broad an audience as possible. All of the authors involved in this volume, students and professionals, have taken this obligation seriously.

The general research framework used at Tijeras Pueblo is explained more fully in the first chapter of this volume. Each of the following chapters is preceded by a brief introduction in which I summarize or highlight the contribution of the chapter to the general research issues. Each of the analytical chapters proceeds in the way that our research is conducted. Thus, a model or theoretical construct, is developed on the basis of current anthropological understanding of human behavior. The models themselves are, by necessity, modified in order to reflect the various cultural and natural processes that prevent the archaeological record from being a clear mirror of the past behavior we wish to understand. Archaeology is a relatively young science, and there is a great deal we do not yet know concerning the ways in which objects are introduced into the archaeological record, the preservation of certain kinds of objects, and how the recovery of items by archaeologists may distort our view of the past. The problems involved in interpreting data are emphasized in the chapters that follow. The development of the models and their modification provide direction both for the analysis that was carried out and for the interpretations that the authors feel comfortable in making.

A further word about the models is in order. The research presented here may strike many readers as being highly materialistic in orientation. There are no chapters on the aesthetic values of the prehistoric peoples we are studying. Nor are there chapters on their religious beliefs or their thoughts. As anthropologists, we are all concerned with viewing human behavior holistically, and it is not a lack of interest in these topics that prevents their discussion here. Rather, the methods archaeologists currently have at their disposal for interpreting the past are much better developed for the material and subsistence realms of human behavior than for the aesthetic and ideational realms. When dealing with prehistoric communities, we have of course, no contemporary written accounts of belief systems. There are only the artifactual remains

3. Mosaic inlay of turquoise, hematite, and shell found in a kiva (room 64) at Tijeras Pueblo. The symbolic meaning of the mosaic is not known.

that reflect aesthetics and ideology (Figure 3). Although these may impress us or appeal to us, we lack the cultural context to interpret them.

If there are genetic descendants of the occupants of Tijeras Pueblo, they are most likely among the modern Rio Grande Pueblo Indians of New Mexico. These people recognize some basic similarities between structures and objects found at Tijeras and those in use at their communities. But it has been five hundred years since Tijeras Pueblo was abandoned, and the cultural context of life for the modern Pueblos has changed dramatically as these people have adapted first to Hispanic and later to Anglo cultural ways. The Rio Grande Pueblos exhibit a wonderfully complex adjustment that has enabled them to retain a good deal of their past life ways and to participate in the twentieth century American society. Nevertheless, it is unwise to consider the contemporary Pueblos either as "living fossils" or as perfect analogs through which to interpret the ways of their ancestors.

There are many individuals and institutions who have aided the research discussed here, and it is impossible to credit them all. I am particularly grateful for the support and interest of the New Mexico Department of Finance and Administration, State Planning Division, Historic Preservation Program; the cooperation of the Osteology Laboratory of the Department of Anthropology, University of New Mexico; the Laboratory of Tree-ring Research, University of Arizona; the Museum of Southwestern Biology, University of New Mexico; the Maxwell Museum of Anthropology, University of New Mexico; and the United States Forest Service, Southwestern Regional Office, Albuquerque. All field school students and staff who were involved in the Tijeras program deserve my wholehearted thanks, as do the men and women of the Sandia Ranger Station. I gratefully acknowledge Jenny Jensen's editorial work, and her periodic assistance in helping me regain my sanity.

L. S. C.

1

The Setting

Linda S. Cordell

Tijeras Canyon is a natural route of travel between the plains of eastern New Mexico and the Rio Grande Valley (Figure 4). The resources of the canyon are those that are attractive to people passing through: water at Tijeras Creek and at various seeps and springs; wood for fuel; and numerous sheltered locations to camp. The physical attributes of the canyon and surrounding mountains would also have made it an attractive place for the hunters and gatherers of the past. In temperate latitudes, these settings provide more diversity in potential plant and animal foods than do settings of lower topographic relief.

Various edible cacti and grasses that yield edible seeds occur at low elevations in the canyon, as do cottontails, jackrabbits, other small mammals, lizards, snakes, and birds. At slightly higher elevations, piñon-juniper woodland is characteristic. Piñon nuts, acorns, juniper berries and bark, and the fruits of understory plants, such as hackberry, barberry, and wild cherry, are available, as are mule deer, rabbits, wild turkeys and other animals. Higher still, yellow pine, Douglas fir, and aspen occur, often bordering open meadows. Bighorn sheep inhabited rugged, mountainous terrain, and antelope could be found in the larger grassy

1

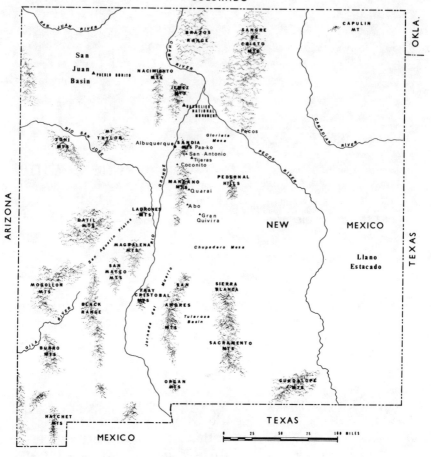

COLORADO

4. Map of New Mexico showing mountain ranges, major drainages, and selected archaeological sites.

upland valleys (Naylor 1964; Findley et al. 1975; Cordell 1977a). The local variations in elevation, and therefore temperature, also extend the length of time during which some edible plants ripen. The gathering of some food plants could therefore be extended over a period of several weeks without necessitating travel over great distances.

Nevertheless, the same conditions that encourage the diversity of flora and fauna inhibit the abundance of any one food source. Differences in elevations, exposure, soil type, and distance from water prevent the development of large, pure stands of plants capable of supporting a great number of large animals or aggregated human communities. Thus, prior to the cultivation of domestic crops, we would expect Tijeras Canyon to have been a favorable setting for small numbers of hunters and gatherers but one that could not have supported even seasonal aggregates of very many people.

Horticulture creates and maintains relatively pure stands of food resources. The labor necessary to clear land, till it, cultivate, and maintain it is more than that required to hunt and gather the naturally available food; however, domestic crops can support more people per hectare of land than can wild food resources (Spooner 1972; Boserup 1965). Agriculture therefore requires and can sustain larger, aggregated human groups. The food crops planted in the Southwest, prior to European contact, were maize, beans, and squash. These had been domesticated in central Mexico about five thousand years before they became important in the diet of southwestern peoples (MacNeish 1971). At first, the prehistoric inhabitants of the Southwest made limited use of domestic crops while continuing the mobile, eclectic subsistence activities of hunting and gathering. Perhaps green corn was first harvested and roasted primarily to enable people to survive the lean time of year before wild food crops were mature. It has been suggested that major dependence on agriculture in the Pueblo Southwest did not take place until regional population levels became too high to permit continued dependence on wild food sources. In view of the relatively greater amount of labor investment agriculture entails, we would not expect societies to rely on cultivated crops until their numbers both permitted and required them to do so (Boserup 1965; Binford 1968).

Tijeras Canyon is not especially well suited to the crops planted by the Anasazi, the term archaeologists use to refer to prehistoric Pueblo peoples. Corn generally needs a growing season of at least 120 days under favorable moisture conditions. In the semiarid Southwest, it matures more slowly (Hack 1942). Over a recent ten-year period, mean annual precipitation in Tijeras Canyon was 36.17 cm. As one goes higher into the mountains, rainfall increases while the growing season is shortened (Figure 5). Most precipitation falls during the winter, when it has no direct effect on maturing agricultural crops. The spring months of April, May, and June are virtually without rain, which means that crops must tap ground moisture for germination. Local soil conditions vary in

5. View of Tijeras Pueblo (foreground) with Sandia Mountains in the background. Note changes in vegetation as elevation increases.

their water retention capabilities. Summer thunderstorms usually begin about mid-July and may last until the beginning of September. These storms provide the moisture necessary for the maturation of crops, but very heavy rains can damage both crops and soil (U.S. Department of Commerce 1974; Naylor 1964; Cordell 1977a, 1977b). Several seeps and springs in the canyon area could provide water for crops, but these occur primarily where the soil is poor. Tijeras Creek, the most abundant source of water, runs through the canyon bottom. There, despite the relatively low elevation, the growing season may be inadequate, because, in both spring and fall, cold air moves into the canyon confines. The frost-free period in the canyon bottom ranged from 105 to 114 days over a recent ten-year interval (Naylor 1964; Cordell 1977a).

Possibly as early as A.D. 900, and certainly by 1200, there were a number of small year round agricultural villages established in the canyon. By about 1300, most of these communities were abandoned and two large villages were established, probably by those who were already living in the canyon. Tijeras Pueblo, one of the large villages, was inhabited until about 1425. San Antonio, the other large village, seems to have been inhabited intermittently until the 1600s. One other neighboring large village, Paa-ko, in a high valley setting between San Antonio and the Cerrillos Hills, was also intermittently occupied about the same time as San Antonio (Cordell 1977b; Lambert 1954). Given the difficulties of predictably producing sufficient food supplies to feed the inhabitants of these villages, we would expect site abandonment to be a common phenomenon.

From about 1594 until the recent period, the number of year-round settlements in the canyon declined rather dramatically. Prior to the establishment of Hispanic towns, the canyon was used as a camping place by the Apache (Oakes 1978). The original Hispanic communities were founded, in part, to protect the growing population of the Rio Grande from unexpected raids by mounted and armed Indians. Even after the raiders had been subdued and the settlers could turn to farming and herding, these pursuits alone were never sufficient to provide economic security. In addition to ranching, the villagers engaged in wage labor, timbering, and mining (Swadesh 1976, 1977). (See Figure 6.)

6. Wagon loads of firewood drawn through Tijeras Canyon in the 1920s.

THE PROBLEM

Our research focuses on understanding and documenting the ways in which human societies adapt to the difficulties and uncertainties of living in the precarious environment of the canyon. We want to understand how people have coped with economic adversity over long periods of time. In general, we conceive of two broad classes of adaptive responses that societies use to contend with less than ideal environmental situations. These classes, referred to here as *technological change* and *social change*, are our analytical categories, and we do not wish to suggest that either one is ever pursued to the exclusion of the other, or that people conceive of them as distinct categories of action.

For our purposes, *technological change* can include developing or importing new crops, using more efficient storage containers, building irrigation works, hunting larger animals, or inventing more effective hunting weapons. *Social change* comprises any adjustments in the way groups of people are organized, such as living in larger communities in order to provide a larger pool of labor for cooperative tasks or to increase the number of people that could conveniently share in the harvest or rewards of the hunt. Social change also includes the formation of more efficient task groups, such as bringing together a large number of hunters to surround a herd of antelope. Another very important kind of social change is the formation of an expanded network of social ties through trade or through intermarriage. Once such ties have been developed, the groups involved generally assume responsibilities for assisting each other.

In order to describe the adaptive responses societies pursued in the past, we approach the archaeological data with specific questions that often require elaborate analyses. For example, in trying to determine changes in trade alliances, we must examine those objects that were imported and be able to document precisely where they were made. The essays in this book develop themes of analysis and interpretation that were used to study the behavioral changes made in Tijeras Canyon. As most of these analyses are relatively new to archaeology, we believe it is important to explain them in detail. With a full understanding of the methods used, and the nature of archaeological data, our interpretations can be fairly evaluated.

The Archaeological Data

In the following essays, a number of specific archaeological sites are discussed. Tijeras Pueblo, San Antonio, and Paa-ko are among those that have been mentioned. As an introduction to the comparative analyses, a brief chronological summary of the prehistory of the Tijeras Canyon area, and the data on which this has been based, is presented here.

The term *PaleoIndian* refers to the first inhabitants of the Americas, the remote ancestors of modern American Indians, who crossed from Siberia into North America during the Late Pleistocene (ca. 30,000 years ago). Although the camps of PaleoIndians have been found in numerous places in the Rio Grande Valley (Judge 1973), no camps of this period have been found in Tijeras Canyon proper. It is likely that PaleoIndians did visit and use the canyon, because Sandia Cave (Hibben 1941), a PaleoIndian campsite, is in the vicinity. But it is possible that open campsites within the canyon confines would be obscured by heavy alluvial deposits.

About 7,000 years ago, when the Southwest had become increasingly dry, a way of life that archaeologists refer to as the *Archaic* was pursued. During the first part of the Archaic, hunting and gathering were the exclusive subsistence activities. During the later part of the Archaic, groups in the Southwest adopted corn but remained primarily hunters and gatherers (Irwin-Williams 1967, 1973). One Archaic site was recorded during the surveys of Tijeras Canyon, but it was not excavated and we have no information about it to include in our analyses (Snow 1972; Blevins and Joiner 1978; Oakes 1978). Numerous Archaic projectile points have been found in Tijeras Canyon, but these are in private collections and have not been used in our studies. The presence of the points and the site do, however, support our contention that the canyon would have been a favorable locality for small groups of hunters and gatherers.

The oldest excavated Anasazi site in Tijeras Canyon is the Big Boulder site (LA 14258), reported by Oakes (1978) for the Museum of New Mexico. The site consisted of two contiguous semicircular pithouses with associated outside hearths and work areas. Ceramics from this site indicate that it was inhabited at about A.D. 700. Earlier pithouses have been excavated west of Albuquerque (Frisbie 1968), and some sites west of Albuquerque date to about the same time as the Big Boulder site (Frisbie 1968; Reinhart 1967; Allen and McNutt 1955; Schorsch 1962; Vytlacil and Brody 1968; Vivian and Clendenen 1965; Skinner 1965). There is no certainty that people were living in Tijeras Canyon year-round by A.D. 700. The Big Boulder site yielded both trough-shaped and slab-shaped metates, indicating that seed processing was one activity carried out there. Unfortunately, the remains of fauna were too fragmentary for them to be precisely identified and are not included in our comparative sample. The Big Boulder site lacked a compact refuse deposit, and partly for that reason, it was suggested that the site was used for temporary, perhaps seasonal, habitation (Oakes 1978).

Sites in Tijeras Canyon that date between about A.D. 900 and A.D. 1250 are known primarily through survey and not from excavation, although sites that were first inhabited in about A.D. 1200 and continued to be inhabited into the 1300s have been excavated. Among the latter are the Dinosaur Rock site (LA 14857) (Oakes 1978) and Coconito (LA 10794). These sites, about a mile apart on gentle slopes immediately above the floodplain of Tijeras Creek, date from about A.D. 1250 to A.D. 1325. They appear to have been relatively small communities situated adjacent to good agricultural land.

The Dinosaur Rock site comprised six rectangular rooms with well-made floors. Three jacal (mud and twig) structures south of the rooms were excavated. The rectangular rooms lacked hearths and much cultural debris whereas the jacal structures each contained a hearth, faunal remains, corn, and other food debris. The excavator (Oakes 1978) suggested that the rectanglar rooms were used primarily for storage whereas the jacal structures were living areas, a common pattern in the Anasazi Southwest.

Coconito is architecturally more complex. The site consisted of about eleven rectangular surface rooms, associated jacal structures, and three nearly rectangular pithouses. The various structures are not contemporary, but the site seems to span a relatively short period of time during which there was considerable architectural modification. At this writing, a complete report of Coconito is not available; however, some of the faunal remains and ceramics are included in our analyses (Young this volume; Warren this volume).

The data from the Dinosaur Rock and Coconito sites, as well as the locations of contemporary sites documented only through site survey, suggest that these communities may represent the first year-round use of the canyon by villagers practicing agriculture. The abundance of storage space at the Dinosaur Rock site may have been necessary to provide enough food for winter in addition to seed corn for the following spring planting. Anderson (1977) has shown that the position of Coconito allowed the maximum collection of solar energy which would have been an advantage during the winter months. Finally, two studies (Blevins and Joiner 1977; Oakes 1978) suggest that between A.D. 1275 and A.D. 1325, there were many small communities in Tijeras Canyon. These are primarily on or adjacent to alluvial soils, at low elevations, and close to land watered by stream runoff (Oakes 1978:4).

Although we do not know where the villagers of this time had been living before settling in Tijeras Canyon, it seems likely that they came from close by, probably the Rio Grande Valley or the foothills of the Manzano Mountains, and may well have been the descendants of those who had previously used the canyon on a seasonal basis. There are no data that would suggest that the villagers represent a migration from the San Juan Basin (to the northwest) or any other remote area. They probably settled the canyon because they were familiar with it, and because agricultural land was becoming scarce elsewhere. They seem to have selected sites to inhabit that offered relatively good areas both to farm and to live in during cold winters.

By 1325, or slightly earlier, many of the small habitation sites in the canyon were abandoned, and population was aggregated at Tijeras Pueblo and San Antonio, both certainly year-round communities. The full extent of San Antonio is not known, because only the portion of the site that was in danger of being destroyed by highway construction was excavated by the Museum of New Mexico. We do know that in the early 1300s Tijeras Pueblo comprised about two hundred rooms (Figure 7). These were distributed in houseblocks arranged in a loose circle that was open to the north. A very large round kiva, an underground ceremonial room, nearly 21 m. in diameter was built in the center of the community (Figure 7). Although most of the rooms were made of adobe and jacal, the kiva walls were double courses of large stone blocks. We cannot know what ceremonies took place in the kiva, but in view of the amount of labor necessary to construct it, we believe the

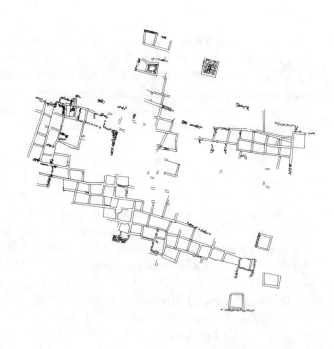

Scale
⊏⊓⊓⊓⊐
←20 ft.→

7. Map of the early rooms at Tijeras Pueblo. Note large circular kiva and open spaces among room blocks.

activities that did take place there were of great importance to the villagers and may have included participation by members of surrounding communities, such as San Antonio.

During the late 1300s Tijeras Pueblo was partially abandoned. Rooms fell into disrepair and adobe walls left exposed, weathered into the ground. A new, smaller pueblo was built over portions of the old structure. The new pueblo was confined to the southern part of the site. Houses were arranged in a U-shape, open to the east, surrounding a plaza. The old circular kiva was abandoned, and a rectangular kiva was built facing the plaza on the western side of the site (Figure 8). The new village contained only about one hundred rooms. These, as well as the kiva, were made of adobe. By about 1425, Tijeras Pueblo was completely abandoned (Cordell 1975, 1977a, 1977b). There is no evidence that either abandonment was the result of hostile attack.

The pattern evidenced by the prehistoric communities in Tijeras Canyon—beginning with dispersed, small villages, followed by large aggregated villages, and eventually by abandonment—is a familiar one in Anasazi prehistory. Many archaeologists today believe that the pattern represents the initial expansion of agriculture into areas where obtaining crops is not reliable. Although this argument appears to be theoretically sound, support for it or refutation of it requires evidence that is difficult to obtain and to evaluate. Some of the difficulties are emphasized in the following essays; however, the record of prehistoric and historic adaptation to Tijeras Canyon is, in many ways, a miniature version of changes that characterized the Southwest as a whole.

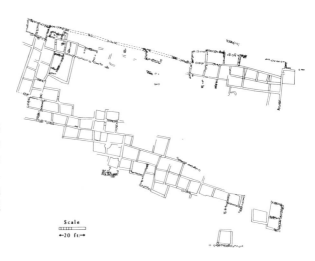

8. Map of late rooms at Tijeras Pueblo. Note contiguous room blocks and east oriented plaza. The kiva associated with this occupation is labelled Room 64.

Scale
←20 ft→

2

A World View
of Agriculture

*Dana Anderson
and Yvonne Oakes*

EDITOR'S INTRODUCTION

In order to interpret prehistoric cultural adaptations, archaeologists generally rely on knowledge of human behavior in the contemporary world. Some archaeologists adapt behavioral models from biological ecology, locational geography, economics, and other fields. Other models may be derived from ethnographic data compiled by cultural anthropologists. Ethnographic data may be used in two ways. The first involves examining certain aspects of behavior that are of theoretical interest to the archaeologist as these occur in a large, world-wide sample of societies. The second, more common, use of ethnographic data involves selecting one or a few societies that are considered appropriate analogs for the prehistoric cultures the archaeologist wants to understand.

In this chapter, Anderson and Oakes use the first method. They examine ethnographic data from a world-wide sample of agricultural societies. The authors are particularly concerned with the relationships among community size, the degree of dependence on agriculture, and the intensity with which agriculture is practiced. Their approach is based on the assumption that these factors are generally related to climate. They explore patterning in climate and three cultural variables of interest. The ethnographic data are used to develop a series of expectations that have implications for Tijeras Pueblo.

L. S. C.

————————◄◆►————————

That there is more order in the world than appears at first sight is not discovered till the order is looked for. (Sigwart, in Hanson 1958:204)

In this chapter, we examine certain characteristics of agricultural societies. Our approach is to understand the adaptive problems faced by nonindustrial agriculturalists around the world. The global perspective suggests particular insights into the problems common to the societies studied and the behaviors that are frequent solutions to these problems. The general observations then permit us to develop specific suggestions relating to Tijeras Pueblo.

Although we might have looked at a variety of social, political, or economic characteristics of agricultural peoples, we have concentrated on relationships among variation in the natural environment, population density, and the intensity of labor invested in agriculture. Our rationale for examining these relationships derives from their importance in current anthropological inquiry relating to the origins of agriculture (e.g. Boserup 1965; Cohen 1977; Reed 1977). The source of our data about agriculturalists throughout the world is Murdock's *Ethnographic Atlas* (1967), a work that was designed to facilitate cross-cultural research.

Comparative studies are fundamental to anthropology. The Human Area Resource Files and the *Ethnographic Atlas* (Murdock 1967), which synthesize ethnographic information, are important tools in research in cultural anthropology. With a few exceptions (e.g. Flannery 1972; Binford 1980), however, archaeologists have made little use of the resources of cross-cultural studies in order to explore correlations in behavioral patterns from the most general perspective. The reluctance of archaeologists to adopt a cross-cultural research strategy based on ethnographic data may, in part, derive from the argument that the range of behavior recorded among contemporary societies is not entirely representative of past behavior before economies of scale dominated the world. This objection undoubtedly has some truth, but it does not negate the usefulness of studying relationships that are at work in the modern world and applying our understanding of these relationships to the past.

THE NATURAL ENVIRONMENT, POPULATION PRESSURE, DEPENDENCE ON AGRICULTURE, AND AGRICULTURAL TECHNOLOGY

One focus of research and debate in contemporary archaeology has been the attempt to explain why man, in various parts of the world, became a farmer rather than continue the ways of a hunting and gathering subsistence (e.g. Reed 1977; Willey and Sabloff 1980). It was generally believed that hunters and gatherers put more time and energy into food procurement than do farmers. Recent studies, however, show that hunters and gatherers work fewer man-hours per year than simple agriculturalists (Lee and DeVore 1966; Harris 1971). In addition, Ester Boserup (1965) showed that as some societies increase the productivity of their agricultural technology (by such means as shortening fallow periods), the amount of labor required to raise that productivity is disproportionate to the return. That is, more food is made available at a higher cost per unit of energy. This is true for many agricultural systems like our own, where the energy we put into agriculture, in the form of fossil fuels, exceeds the energy output in crops. Boserup's (1965) study suggests that to increase agricultural production, or to begin agriculture in the first place, must be viewed as a response to particular problems man faces.

The recent arguments in the archaeological literature concerning agricultural production have centered on defining specific problems man has encountered that lead to farming and the intensification of farming. At present, the two most visible schools of thought on the subject are (1) advocates of population pressure explanations (e.g. Cohen 1977) and (2) those who emphasize the reduction of subsistence risk (e.g. Sanders and Webster 1978). The first group of scholars view agricultural production and intensification as a response to local or world-wide population buildup. People eventually could not be supported by naturally available foods. Then, according to this scenario, some people were forced into developing agriculture, despite the fact that agriculture requires more time and energy than hunting and gathering.

Other scholars have noted that in some environments, particularly those characterized by unpredictable rainfall, labor invested in agricultural intensification may multiply productivity many times. For example, irrigation will produce a more efficient system as well as lowering the risk of depending on unpredictable precipitation. The change to irrigation will, however, entail great social adjustments (Sanders and Webster 1978). Without going into the details of these debates, we do take the position that all societies are conservative and resist major change of any kind until the alternatives to change are intolerable.

Consideration of either population pressure or risk reduction requires examination of different physical environments. In order to explore population pressure, a measure such as population density is necessary. But population pressure should occur at lower population densities in some environments than in other, more benign environments. The amount of risk or unpredictability of subsistence can be measured only with respect to particular environmental features such as rainfall or the length of the growing season.

In our opinion, the following assumptions can be made about man's adaptation to any natural environment: (1) local physical environments offer different problems requiring different responses from man; (2) only a limited variety of responses is possible in any given environment and (3) in a broad sense, men living in similar environments will solve problems, including population pressure, in similar ways. The focus of our study, then, is the relationship among population pressure, agricultural dependency, and agricultural labor intensification under varying environmental conditions.

SELECTION OF VARIABLES AND MEASUREMENTS

Environmental Variables

The particular environmental variables we examine reflect the problems they would pose to a society with any dependence on agriculture. They are a measure of the relative length of the growing season (Effective Temperature) and the availability of water (Aridity Index). Originally, we saw availability of water as a function of rainfall, but further research showed that most of the societies we looked at grow crops under conditions of an annual water deficit. The problem for these agriculturalists, then, is overcoming an insufficient water supply. We therefore created a relative aridity index that begins at zero (sufficient water) and measures the water deficit in millimeters (Figure 9). Our use of a world sample of agricultural societies required that we select environmental measures that are comparable on a global basis.

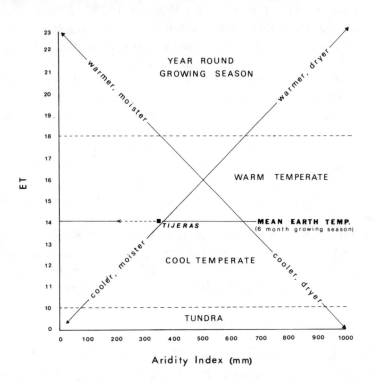

Aridity Index (mm)

9. *Environmental Model:*

Effective Temperature (ET)

(measure of growing season)

1. ET of less than 10 is not suitable for most plant growth.
2. ET 14 is the mean earth temperature.
3. ET between 10 and 14 is a cool zone with a relatively short growing season.
3. ET between 14 and 18 is a warm zone with a longer growing season.
4. ET 18 is the point at which the growing season is year round.
6. ET between 18 and 23 indicates hotter temperatures.

Aridity Index

1. At zero, there is no water deficit.
2. As the aridity index increases, water becomes a limiting factor for unassisted plant growth.

Climatological data are general indicators of potential plant growth and are therefore critically important to agriculturalists. Climatological data can be used as approximations of the agricultural potential of an area for nonindustrialized farmers. It is not necessary to use every climatic factor if a few limit the effect of all the others. For example, plant growth stops when either a low or high temperature threshold is exceeded, regardless of light, moisture, or available nutrients (Chang 1968:75). Similarly, available moisture is a limiting factor. We selected temperature and rainfall, or precipitation, as the environmental variables because of their known effect on plant growth and because both are easily measured, and have been measured, throughout the world more systematically than any other climatic data.

For each society in our sample (Figures 10, 11, and discussion below), we computed mean annual precipitation and monthly temperatures (Wernstedt 1972) by interpolating from three recording stations located within 30 miles of that society. Elevation was used as a check in order to eliminate those stations at widely different elevations from the point of interest, since this would have made the interpolation suspect. When it was not possible to obtain the necesary data in order to interpolate the local climate, the society was dropped from the sample.

Precipitation data can be used in two ways. An actual measure of precipitation is an indicator of plant growth, but by itself can be misleading. Solar radiation, or the intensity and duration of sunlight, can modify the amount of moisture available for plant growth. One of the major ways solar radiation limits moisture is through evapotranspiration, or the combination of evaporation of water from the plant and the surrounding soil, and transpiration, the process by which the plant draws water from the soil to be vaporized from the leaf surfaces. In order adequately to describe and predict plant growth both actual rainfall and evapotranspiration should be measured. Two measures of evapotranspiration are necessary to predict gross plant production—potential and actual evapotranspiration. Potential evapotranspiration is that which would take place in a plant community if the water supply were unlimited. Actual evapotranspiration is that which actually takes place when the availability of water is limited, as it is in those areas of the world from which our sample of societies was taken. The combination of solar radiation and rainfall produces a mea-

10. List of the sample of agricultural societies used in the comparative study. The societies were selected from those included in the *Ethnographic Atlas*.

North America
Chippewa	(Ontario, Manitoba, and Minnesota)
Hidatsa	(North Dakota)
Iroquois	(New York)
Pawnee	(Nebraska)
Omaha	(Nebraska)
Navajo	(Arizona and New Mexico)
Cherokee	(North Carolina)
Kaibab	(Arizona)
Wichita	(Oklahoma)
Creek	(Georgia)
Maricopa	(Arizona)
Natchez	(Louisiana)

Mexico
Yaqui
Huichol
Tarahumara
Mixe
Tarasco

South America and Central America
Quiche	(Guatemala)	
Bribri	(Costa Rica	Panama?)
Inca	(Peru)	
Mapuche	(Argentina)	
Lenca	(Honduras)	
Yupa	(Columbia)	

Europe
Basques	(Andorra)

Africa
Kissi	
Kabyle	(Algeria)
Barea	(Ethiopia)
Tswana	(Botswana)
Anuak	(Sudan)
Arusi	(Ethiopia)

Ga	(Ghana)
Nyoro	(Uganda)
Kikuyu	(Kenya)
Burundi	(Ruanda)
Tanala	(Malagasy)
Yombe	(Congo and Angola)
Gogo	(Tanzania)
Mbundu	(Angola)
Chewa	(Malawi)
Swazi	(Mozambique)
Wolof	(Senegal)
Guanche	(Canary Islands)

Asia

Druze	(Israel)
Manchu	(China)
Cherkess	(Soviet Union)
Ainu	(Japan)
Gheg	(Albania)
Hazara	(Afghanistan)
Pahari	(India)
Sherpa	(Nepal)
Garo	(India)
Sindhi	(Pakistan)
Santal	(India)
Atayal	(Taiwan)
Chakma	(Bangladesh)
Burmese	(Burma)
Coorg	(India)
Mnong Gar	(South Vietnam)
Chenchu	(India)

Oceania

Sagada Igorot	(Philippines)
Siamese	(Thailand)
Chamorro	(Mariana Islands)
Sugbuhanon	(Philippines)
Sinhalese	(Ceylon)
Senoi	(Malaysia)
Javanese	(Java)
Balinese	(Bali)
Belu	(Portuguese Timor)

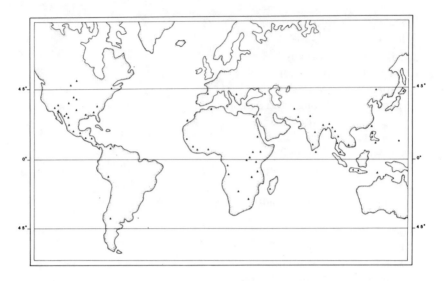

11. World map showing locations of the societies used in the comparative study.

sure of actual evapotranspiration. If actual precipitation falls below potential evapotranspiration, there is a water deficit.

Rainfall and solar radiation were used to arrive at the index of relative aridity. In other studies (Tuan 1973; Chang 1968), rainfall is simply subtracted from potential evapotranspiration to arrive at an annual water deficit. However, we used the difference between potential evapotranspiration and actual evapotranspiration, because the latter represents rainfall corrected for runoff. Runoff is computed to estimate whether or not soil moisture (effected by solar radiation) is low enough to allow absorption of new rainfall, or whether that rain will become runoff, joining a drainage system. This distinction is important when one is trying to rely solely on rainfall to water crops. In effect, our figures for annual water deficit are higher than those using potential evapotranspiration minus rainfall, because not all rainfall moisture becomes available in the soil for plants. Our aridity index is potential evapotranspiration minus actual evapotranspiration measured in millimeters per year.

Effective Temperature or ET (Bailey 1960), which uses data on the coldest and warmest month in an area, was used as a measure of the growing season. ET also expresses the variation caused by latitude and altitude, both of which influence temperature and the length of the growing season.

Cultural Variables

The three cultural variables of interest to us are population density, or the number of people per unit of land, the amount of dependence a society places upon agriculture, and the intensity of labor involved in agricultural practices. Not all of these variables are recorded as separate entities in the *Ethnographic Atlas* (Murdock 1967). The Atlas does, however, include categories that allowed us to measure these factors indirectly.

In order to measure population density, we combined information Murdock (1967) listed under the categories of community size and settlement pattern. Community size refers to the average population of local communities derived from census data or other evidence, and is grouped into discrete categories (Murdock 1967: 51). We combined the discrete categories into two major divisions. Thus, we recorded community size as low for all societies with less than 200 persons in each local community, and high when community size is 200 or more persons.

Murdock (1967:51) included two variables in his categories of settlement pattern. These are the relative permanency of communities and the compactness or dispersion of homesteads on the landscape. We consider that societies in which communities could be fully migratory, nomadic, or seminomadic probably reflected general conditions of low population density. Using our dichotomy of community size and a dichotomy between impermanent and permanent settlement patterns, as recorded in the *Atlas*, we assigned communities to either a low-population-density category or a high-population-density category. A few groups had permanent settlements but very small communities. These were included in the low-population-density category. Tijeras Pueblo would be an example of this kind of community (See Table 1 for a comparison of the *Atlas* categories and our definition of population density.) In order to measure agricultural practices, we recorded information from two categories listed in the *Atlas:* (1) the "Dependence on Agriculture" expressed as a percentage of total subsistence activities (Murdock 1967:46–47 and Table 1), and (2) Intensity of Agriculture (Murdock 1967:51 and Table 1).

THE SAMPLE

Murdock's *Atlas* includes information on 826 societies. At first, we limited the sample to include only those groups that depend on

TABLE 1. Use of Murdock's Classification System to Create
Categories for World Agricultural Study

Dependence on Agriculture (Murdock)	Intensity of Agriculture* (Murdock)	Settlement Pattern (Murdock)	Community Size (Murdock)	Population Density
0–35%	Extensive (low)			
		Migratory Seminomadic; Semisedentary; Impermanent, compact	Fewer than 50 to 199 (low)	Low
				Low
36–65%	Intensive (high)			
		Neighborhoods, separate hamlets; Permanent compact; Complex; Sedentary	200 to more than 1,000 (high)	Medium and high
66–100%	Intensive with irrigation (high)	Sedentary	200– 50,000 (high)	High

*Definitions of Agricultural Intensity (after Murdock)

Extensive =   New fields cleared annually and cultivated for 1–2 years followed by a long fallow period. (Ex: Jicarilla Apache)

Intensive =   Permanent fields using fertilizers, crop rotation, or other means to eliminate fallow periods. (Ex: Acoma)

Intensive with irrigation =   Same as intensive, but largely dependent on irrigation (water control). (Ex: Hopi)

Examples:

Jicarilla Apache   0–35%, Extensive, mobile (low), no community size noted, low population density.

Acoma   66–100%, Intensive, sedentary, > 1000 persons (high), high population density.

Hopi   66–100%, Intensive with irrigation, sedentary, 200–400 persons (medium-high), high population density.

agriculture for any portion of their subsistence requirements. The field was further narrowed by eliminating any society whose primary crops were not grains such as maize, wheat, rye, millet, or sorghum. This criterion was applied because the labor and technological requirements for crops that differ structurally, such as tubers and melons, could affect agricultural intensity and social structure independently of the variables we are interested in. The societies examined were chosen according to the stratified random sampling method recommended by Murdock (1967). Finally, some societies were eliminated from the sample because it was not possible to obtain the necessary data on climate. Our final sample contained the 75 societies listed in Figure 10 and mapped in Figure 11.

MODELS AND PATTERNS

Our concern is to determine if there are any general patterns in the way simple farmers solve particular problems. Therefore, we have identified problems of interest and formed these problems into an environmental model not unlike a game board. Figure 9 shows the environmental rules for the game. The combination of changing growing season and varying water deficit creates zones on the game board as characterized in Figure 12. The upper left-hand corner is a warm, moist zone; the lower righthand half of the board is cool and dry. Between these two areas, all the remaining combinations of available water and growing season form the intermediate area. A player who must support himself by farming will have to apply a different strategy in a warm, moist climate than a player who inhabits a cool, dry zone. There are not an unlimited number of ways to solve these different problems. Rather, it is left up to the player to use different combinations of a few solutions to effect the best strategy. The solutions available to the players include varying the dependency upon agriculture, varying the relative intensity of the farming strategy, and controlling the population densities.

After setting up the game in this manner, we took the 75 agricultural societies (Figures 10 and 11) and found how they solve the stated problems. Keep in mind as you see the distribution of cases across the board that societies in close proximity on the board may be 20,000 miles apart in the real world. Their relative position on the game board reflects the relative comparability of their climates.

In order to reduce the confusion that can result from trying to comprehend all possible combinations of variables at once, we have chosen to hold one or more variables constant while seeing

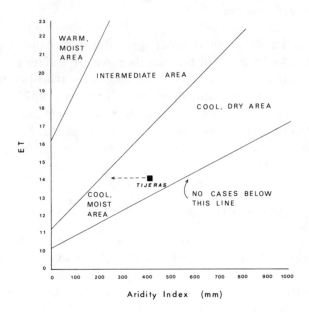

12. Environmental zones of changing growing season and varying water deficit.

how the other variables are differentially used as solutions. When we hold a variable constant, we limit the amount of variation we are viewing at any one time. For instance, we might look at solutions used by low-population-density groups only. Viewing the sets separately allows us to pick up the subtly different solutions and combinations of solutions. After we understand the simpler situations, we can begin to recombine them much as you would build a house with individual bricks. If each brick is adequately formed and properly placed, then upon completion the house will be a solid, functioning unit. In the same patient manner we want to build both a model that describes the world adequately and a theoretical framework that explains what we see. Now for the patterns that are created as these cases apply their strategies.

The lines that separate the categories on our graphs are computed in the same way a topographic map is created. Contours are drawn by connecting points which have the same value. This reduces a three-dimensional subject to a two-dimensional surface. Visualize the ascending categories (36–65 percent is greater than 1–35 percent) as a hill comprised of increasing agricultural dependence. The top of the hill is 100 percent dependence upon farming. Each graph is read in this manner with hills of high values surrounded by valleys of low values.

To begin with we held population density constant at low and then high value to see how the societies in question handled limitations with differing amounts of dependency upon agriculture (Figures 13 and 14).

The fact that the largest area of highest agriculture dependence was totally unused when the population density was low (Figures 13 and 14) suggests that this particular segment poses special problems to farmers. These problems seem to work against use of the area until there are enough people or enough commitment to farming to overcome them. As we go through all the patterns, it will become apparent that when populations become more dense the patterning in this intermediate zone becomes complex and harder for us to understand intuitively in terms of our problem-solving model. This indicates that there are influencing factors in

13. Amount of agricultural dependence in societies with low population densities. In this case, the pattern is distributed in congruence with the environmental zones shown in Figure 12. Societies with some degree of mobility and the small communities depend on agriculture to provide less than 35 percent of their subsistence needs in cool, dry climates. Dependence on agriculture increases to 36–65 percent in the intermediate zone and to 66–100 percent in warm, moist areas.

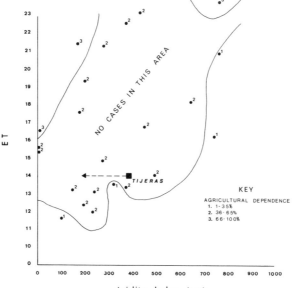

KEY

AGRICULTURAL DEPENDENCE
1. 1-35%
2. 36-65%
3. 66-100%

Aridity Index (mm)

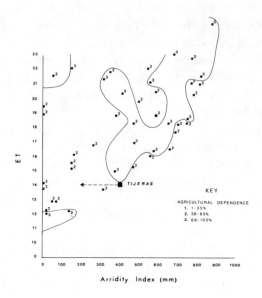

ET

Arridity Index (mm)

KEY

AGRICULTURAL DEPENDENCE
1. 1-35%
2. 36-65%
3. 66-100%

TIJERAS

14. Amount of agricultural dependence in societies with high population densities. In this case, there are more isolated hills of 66–100 percent dependence on agriculture surrounded by large areas of 35–65 percent dependence on agriculture. No societies appear with less than 36 percent dependence on agriculture.

the intermediate area which we are not monitoring. We suggest that rainfall, growing season, and predictability of available water from year to year may be pertinent climatic variables posing specialized problems that threaten the stability of the agricultural system. In other words, if rain falls during the growing season only three out of five years, or if a major drought occurs one out of every three years, a farming society faces special threats to its subsistence stability which it will only risk under certain conditions. One such condition may exist when there are enough people to build and maintain water control systems that can overcome an unpredictable climate. This involves a commitment of time and labor which in turn means that agriculture must supply a large amount of the subsistence needs. Other subsistence pursuits become secondary to the more complex farming strategy.

Each graph in the next series, (Figures 15, 16, and 17) holds population density constant and allows agricultural intensity to vary. Irrigation can be viewed as a particular type of intensive

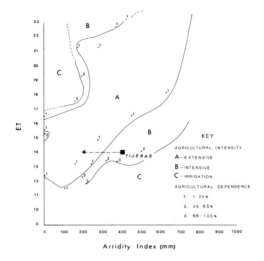

15. Degree of agricultural intensity in societies with low population densities. Agricultural intensity increases as the climate becomes warmer and more moist and as conditions become cooler and drier. The intermediate area is comprised entirely of societies using extensive agricultural strategies.

16. Degree of agricultural dependence in societies with high population densities. This pattern is quite complex. Warm moist areas and cool dry areas are characterized by extensive systems while the intermediate area has a series of hills and troughs of relatively high agricultural intensity.

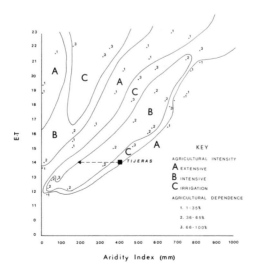

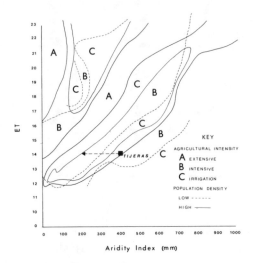

17. Degree of agricultural intensity in societies with high and low population densities. This chart simplifies the patterns in Figures 15 and 16. Intensive and irrigation agricultural strategies are combined into a single category, because Murdock suggests that there may not be a difference in labor costs between the two.

strategy aimed at alleviating certain conditions of water deficiency. The patterns in Figures 16 and 17 are more informative than in Figure 15. As population density increases, more and more of the intermediate area is characterized by intensive strategies, while both the moist, warm zone and the cool, dry zone are not areas of intensive strategies. Figures 18 and 19 each hold population density constant, but compare the patterns of dependency on agriculture and the intensity of agriculture. Table 2 lists the characteristics of, and some generalizations about the patterns in Figures 13 through 19.

In an effort to elucidate the complex situation in the intermediate area we decided to hold the intensity of the farming strategy constant and see how population density is distributed (Figures 20 and 21). Two generalizations are possible from these patterns: (1) as populations grow, intensive strategies spread toward cooler, drier areas from the initial warm, moist zone; and (2) as population density increases in the intermediate zone, intensive strategies come to characterize the entire zone.

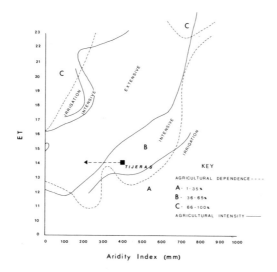

18. Agricultural dependence and intensity in low population areas.

19. Agricultural dependence and intensity in high population areas.

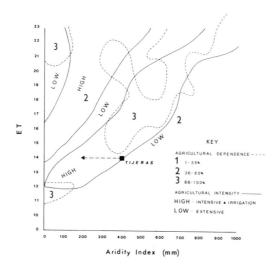

TABLE 2. Holding Population Constant; Varying Agricultural Dependence and Intensity

Hot and Relatively Moist Niches	*Intermediate Area*	*Coolest and Driest Niches*
Low population density: —two cases of intensive agriculture, —more than 150mm A; more than 66% dependence on agriculture	Low population density: —36–65% agricultural dependence and extensive strategy	Low Population density: —dependence on agriculture ranges from less than 35% to less than 65% as the environment becomes warmer and moister —intensity increases as it becomes cooler and dryer until irrigation is necessary with less than 35% dependence
High population density: —more than 36% dependence on agriculture —low intensity until Aridity Index reaches 150mm, where intensity increases	High population density: —irregular pattern of alternating clusters of dependence, 36–65% and 66–100% —alternating clusters of intensity going toward warmer and moister, high—low—high	High population density: —dependence decreases as climate gets cooler and dryer but does not drop below 36%: one niche with cool but moist conditions supports more than 66% dependence —intensity decreases as dependence decreases and the climate becomes cooler and dryer
Generalizations: —intensity increases as aridity increases over 150mm —low population density can depend on agriculture for 66% or more of subsistence needs —high population density can depend on agriculture for more than 66% of needs in hot, moist areas and more than 36% as environment gets cooler and dryer	Generalizations: —although there are clusters, the patterns are not understandable in terms of the climatic variables we used —measuring congruence of growing season and available water would possibly make the situation clearer as would a better measure of population density and mobility	Generalizations: —with cooler and dryer conditions surviving the winter becomes more difficult —low population density can be supported with increasing intensity and less dependence on agriculture —high population densities cannot be supported until conditions become warmer and moister when intensity and dependence increase

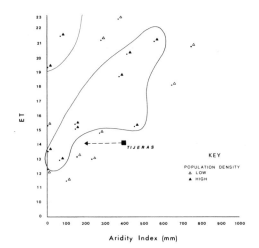

20. Low intensity comparison with high and low populations.

21. High intensity comparison with high and low populations.

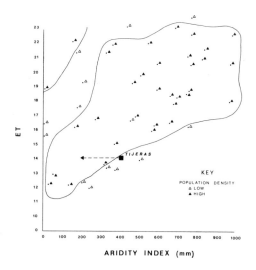

In Figures 22 through 25 agricultural dependence is held constant and population density varies. Societies depending upon farming to supply under 35 percent of their subsistence needs are located predominantly in the cool, dry zone and all have low population densities (Figure 2). In contrast, groups which use crops to supply over 66 percent of their food are predominantly in the warm, dry section of the intermediate zone and, with two exceptions, all have high population densities (Figure 23). Figure 24 shows that these two patterns are almost mutually exclusive: the warm, moist climates are characterized by high population densities with a very high dependence on crops, while the cool, dry area contains groups with low population densities and less dependence upon agriculture. This suggests that our climatic model influences the extremes. When a medium agricultural dependence is graphed, a complex pattern appears in the intermediate area (Figure 25).

When agricultural dependence is held constant, the warm, moist areas appear to support higher population densities and a higher dependence upon farm products with varying degrees of labor. In other words, population pressure may be the problem to be solved by increasing dependence upon crops and increasing intensity, since the climate appears to pose few problems for plant growth. The cool, dry environments seem to support fewer people per unit of land with a subsistence strategy that depends less upon agriculture using varying degrees of labor. In these societies agriculture may be used to buffer the economy for the winter no matter how low the population density. In this case intensification of labor is not designed to feed increasing populations but rather to overcome a climate that is less conducive to plant growth because the additional food is needed even at low population densities.

When agricultural dependence is held constant, the patterns in the intermediate zone for the most part defy generalization. Far from being a straightforward linear relationship among population pressure, increasing dependence upon agriculture, and increasingly intensive strategies, the relationship appears to vary according to the problems to be solved. Population pressure, storage of food over the winter, and combinations of length of growing season and available water seem to influence the dependence on crops and labor intensity under varying population densities in a complex manner not anticipated by our model.

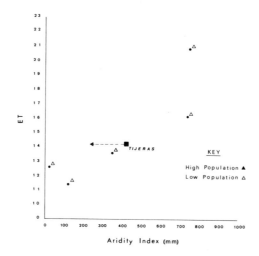

22. Societies that depend on agriculture between 1 and 35 percent comparing high and low population densities.

23. Societies that depend on agriculture between 36 and 65 percent comparing high and low population densities.

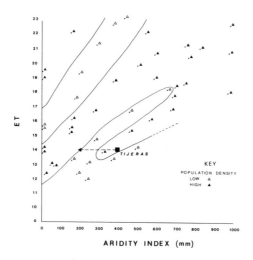

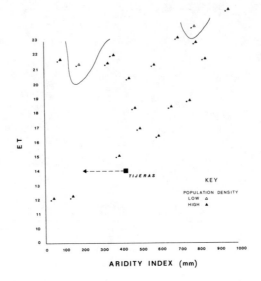

24. Societies that depend on agriculture between 66 and 100 percent comparing high and low population densities.

25. Degree of dependence on agriculture with societies of both high and low population densities.

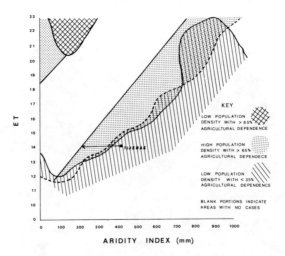

Predictability of moisture and growing season could account for much of this variation and should be studied further.

Another point derives from differences between the low and high population density patterns. The low population density patterns are clearer and easier to interpret in terms of our model than the patterns for high population density, which are more complex. We think the reason is simply that we have isolated an integral unit with the low population density group, and we have not done so in the high. A finer-grained study of the high density category may result in several categories each with less complex patterns than we see when they are all grouped together. Given Murdock's community size category (Table 1) and the number of cases we chose, merging the categories was necessary, because there were too few cases to see a pattern when we tried to subdivide the group. Our model appears to have value in explanation and prediction only for groups with a population of fewer than 200 that are not totally sedentary, or small permanent communities, and for environments that are either relatively moist and warm or are cool and dry.

Work remains to be done to understand the transformations that take place as populations become permanently settled in an area and community size increases. Some of the complex patterns in the high density graphs are caused by groups that have intermediate community sizes and are permanently settled in one spot. Studying such groups in particular may help to answer many of our questions.

TIJERAS CANYON

The modern climate of Tijeras Canyon is in the cool, dry zone (Figure 12). Both water and temperature are critical variables affecting farming in this area. The average rainfall for Tijeras Canyon is 365 mm, but the high incidence of solar radiation in New Mexico, both winter and summer (Tuan et al. 1973:102–3, Figures 43 and 44), creates an annual water deficit of 382 mm. The ET is 14. Today the area is characterized by late summer and early winter rainfall (wettest months are July, August, and October), which is not totally congruent with the relatively short growing season of 134 frost-free days for the growth and maturation of corn. The last frost in spring and the first hard freeze in fall

are unpredictable and can fall as late as May 20 and as early as
October 1. The problem, then, is to plant the seeds when they can
get the necessary moisture during the critical times of germination
and flowering (Chang 1968), but at such a time that they will not
erupt above ground until after the last frost and can mature totally
before the first freeze.

The canyon is relatively narrow with steep rocky sides. It rises
in altitude from 5,600 feet at the west end to 7,000 feet at the east.
Rainfall increases with altitude, but the growing season decreases
accordingly. An arroyo runs the full length of the canyon, and the
associated floodplain and alluvium provide the only cultivable
soils. Springs dot the course of the arroyo and provide water year
round, but have been known to fail (see Cordell and Quintana and
Kayser, this volume). The steep sides of the canyon, which make
up most of the drainage area, cause considerable runoff with high
rainfall, which leads to flooding and arroyo cutting. These same
steep walls create a "canyon" effect where air movement causes
lower temperatures along the arroyo than higher up the canyon
sides. The total effect of these topographical and climatological
characteristics is that today Tijeras Canyon is not a very good
location for farming.

Cordell (this volume, Chapter 3) provides some evidence that
the climate, at least, may have been more amenable to farming in
the past. The 1300s were appreciably more moist than today. It is
not possible, however, to compute an exact annual water deficit
for that time. Instead, on all the graphs we have shown Tijeras
Canyon as it is today with a dashed line leading toward improved
moisture conditions.

In this section we discuss Tijeras Pueblo and the canyon in
terms of changing population density and changing climate, both
of which can cause an imbalance between population and natural
resources. Survey data suggest that Tijeras Canyon was not the
location of residential sites until quite late in time. We do not suggest that the transition from hunters and gatherers to agriculturalists took place in this locality. The first residents were already in-
corporating a little farming into their subsistence strategy,
although there is no direct evidence that the farming was taking
place in Tijeras Canyon proper. During the history of the pre-
Hispanic occupation of Tijeras Canyon, changes in population
density and climate did take place. We will use the cross-cultural
model presented previously to discuss changes through time.

Figures 13 through 25 depict the boundaries of both climatic zones and subsistence strategies. Visualize again a topographic map where the contours represent various altitudes on a two-dimensional surface. Now think of these graphs in the same way, as hills and valleys, with the boundary lines being points we can measure but which really represent a continuum. A society does not suddenly adopt a valley-wide irrigation system when the population density reaches a magic number. The rate of change is slow and accretional and not clearly understood. In order to depict this phenomenon, we have graphed some of the variables from a different perspective (Figure 26).

We have taken slices through the plan maps and have redrawn these slices to depict the height of the hills and valleys. We chose to cut slices through the 400 line on the Aridity Index because this characterizes Tijeras Canyon today, and the 200 line because this is a relatively more moist climate. We wish to show changes that might take place as conditions become wetter. In this case, substantially wetter conditions reduce the risk to an agricultural economy (Figure 12).

By comparing the two indices of aridity and changing population densities, these graphs indicate corresponding changes in agricultural dependence and intensity. Figure 26 shows how changes in climate would affect low population density. As conditions become wetter than today at ET 14 (ET does not vary much until there are drastic changes such as glacial periods) the dependence upon agriculture increases slightly while the intensity of the labor decreases substantially. Under conditions of high population density, the same climatic change results in a slight decrease in dependence on farming while the intensity remains high, which may reflect the higher incidence of alternative resources under wetter conditions. As the climate worsens in the early 1400s, these trends are reversed.

By comparing the graphs in Figure 26 it is possible to look at one Aridity Index at ET 14 and discuss corresponding changes as population density increases. Under the wetter conditions of Aridity 200, as population density increases, dependence upon agriculture stays the same, but the intensity increases from extensive to irrigation—a drastic change. Under dryer conditions, as the population density increases the dependence upon farming increases slightly and the intensity increases less drastically from intensive to irrigation.

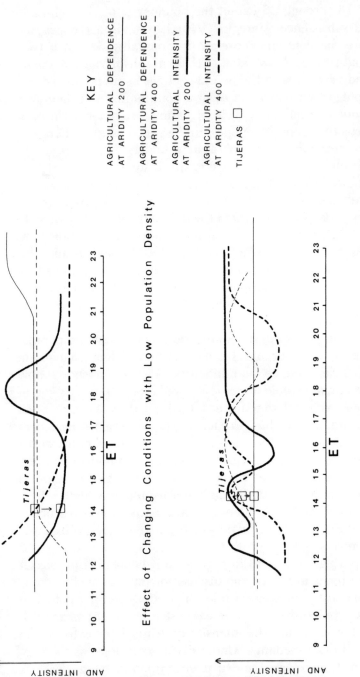

KEY

AGRICULTURAL DEPENDENCE
AT ARIDITY 200 ——————

AGRICULTURAL DEPENDENCE
AT ARIDITY 400 – – – – –

AGRICULTURAL INTENSITY
AT ARIDITY 200 ▬▬▬▬

AGRICULTURAL INTENSITY
AT ARIDITY 400 ▬ ▬ ▬ ▬

TIJERAS □

Effect of Changing Conditions with Low Population Density

ET

INCREASING DEPENDENCE
AND INTENSITY

ET

INCREASING DEPENDENCE
AND INTENSITY

26. Effects of Changing Conditions. This graph was constructed by placing a pointer on the aridity index and following it. Whenever a boundary is encountered, the ET is noted and a change in height is made on the graph. Abrupt changes are then smoothed out to indicate gradual change. At this point in the modeling, the relative steepness of the slope does not imply a difference in rate of change, although this is an impor-

These are the general world-wide patterns, but how do they apply to Tijeras Canyon? The topography and the juxtaposition of springs to arable land limit the possibilities for irrigation; if irrigation were a required response, it would be only partially successful. Intensive strategies are more appropriate, however. Huck (1942) shows how the Hopi stagger the planting time over several weeks and plant in many diverse locations in order to take advantage of many subtle combinations of rainfall and temperature. If all the plants matured, there would be a large surplus, but this rarely happens, so the Hopi keep one to three years' food supply stored in order to offset drastic crop failures. Another way to intensify is to increase the stability of the agricultural system by adding nutrients to the soil with fertilizer or by multiple cropping of complimentary plant species. Also pests can be controlled in order to increase the yield. In the Southern United States and Mesoamerica, turkeys are used to control pests in the fields (L. Binford and R. Santley personal communication 1979). Although few people have pursued the possibility of turkeys used for pest control in the prehistoric Southwest their presence in agricultural sites could indicate such use.

In summary, Tijeras Canyon today is climatologically a high-risk area for agriculture. Although this risk may occasionally have been diminished in the past by periodic decades of higher rainfall, ingenuity and intensified labor strategies have always been necessary to maintain the agricultural dependence at a potential high of 36–65 percent. Other studies (Young, this volume) suggest that stress was placed on faunal resources and indicate a high-starch, low-protein diet (Ferguson, this volume) for some of the population. This evidence suggests that the people in Tijeras Canyon tried to keep their dependence upon farm products as high as possible while under nutritional stress. When the climate began to deteriorate, this already marginal existence was further threatened and rapid changes had to take place.

ACKNOWLEDGMENTS

We thank Lewis R. Binford for sharing with us his thoughts on climatic variables and graphics as an analytical technique. This paper depends heavily on those ideas.

We also thank Jack Bertram for unselfishly sharing with us his considerable graphics skill.

Stephanie Klausner spent several nights helping us get the computer to produce scatter diagrams of our data; we thank her profusely. Finally, thanks are owed to our student colleagues who read and criticized this paper. Their criticisms have helped us produce a better article.

We owe a great deal to Jenny Jensen who rendered our verbiage into English.

3

The Development
of the Tijeras Canyon
Hispanic Communities

Frances Leon (Swadesh) Quintana
and David Kayser

EDITOR'S INTRODUCTION

The archival records and contemporary ethnography of the
Hispanic settlement of the canyon are an additional, and very
rich, source of data on adaptation to Tijeras. In this chapter,
Quintana describes the precarious economic base of the Hispanic
communities, and Kayser contributes data on their agricultural
technology. Their paper provides a detailed case study of one contemporary society that might have been part of Anderson's and
Oakes' world sample. The example is particularly useful since the
Hispanic settlements are, of course, in the same environmental settings as the prehistoric villages under study. It is important to
note, however, that the economic, technological, and political
contexts of the Hispanic settlement were and are very different
from those possible prehistorically. For example, in addition to
corn and beans, the Hispanic settlers cultivated vegetables such as
onions, carrots, and cabbage. Apple and peach orchards were
maintained although their yields were not reliable. Because crops
were unpredictable, livestock was more important than farming;
the sheep, goats, and cattle so critical to the Hispanic economy

were unknown to the Anasazi. The ability of the land grant communities to sustain themselves through periods of poor harvests, raiding, and a declining land base manifest the tenacity and ingenuity of human adaptation.

L.S.C.

———————◀◆▶———————

This paper is an ethnohistorical study of the social and economic conditions of the historic Tijeras Canyon communities. The period of time involved is a long one, beginning with the foundation of an Hispanic frontier settlement in the mid 1700s, and ending with the massive incursion of modern industrial society in the 1900s.

The study is divided into two sections. In the first, Quintana establishes the environmental, economic, and cultural conditions of early historic Tijeras Canyon, traces the ways in which these conditions have changed, and describes the economic and social strategies by which Tijeras Canyon residents have adapted to these conditions. The data for this section were collected from three different sources. Much of the information was compiled from published and unpublished documents, especially those in the Spanish and Mexican archives of New Mexico. This information was then linked with the verbal recollections of many willing and knowledgeable informants from the immediate communities and, to the fullest extent possible, with archaeological data as these data were in the process of being uncovered (Swadesh 1977).

In the second section, Kayser investigates the technological strategies used by Tijeras communities to adapt to the changing economic and ecological situation in the canyon. Once again, the data come from multiple sources. Information on a few of the prehistoric and several of the historic water systems in Tijeras Canyon was collected by archaeological survey. To this was added the available archival and published material on agriculture, hydraulic management, regional climatic cycles, and accounts of the agricultural and livestock activities recollected by informants.

There were many difficulties in assembling and interpreting this information. The archival sources were often incomplete and, while the oral tradition of the Tijeras Canyon communities is strong, place and circumstances tend inevitably to become blurred of time. The disturbance of early features by later construction in over many generations. The identification of possible prehistoric and historic hydraulic features was hindered by the circumstances the same location and by recent extensive earth-modifying activities, such as the construction of highways, utility lines, parking lots, and buildings, has in some instances obliterated the remains of previous systems. Despite these difficulties, it was possible to put together a reasonably coherent history of community development in the Tijeras Canyon area, relating the gradual replacement of prehistoric and early historic Indian communities by Hispanic frontier settlements, and a corresponding change of adaptive technologies.

HISTORY OF SETTLEMENT

The Buffer Community

The colonial Hispanic villages of New Mexico reflected the circumstances that led to their founding, the environmental conditions within which they developed, and the functions that they served.

During the Spanish Colonial period in the Rio Grande area (1696–1821), the government was much concerned with the aggressive activities of nomadic groups such as the Comanche, the Apache, and the Ute. This concern led to a policy of establishing buffer outpost communities to blunt, or even deter, raids on Santa Fe, Albuquerque, and Santa Cruz de la Cañada, the principal settlements of New Mexico.

In the mid 1700s Governor Tomás Veles Cachupín authorized the founding of some early buffer towns—San José de las Trampas in 1751, Nuestra Señora de la Luz, San Fernando y San Blas on the Puerco River in 1753, Abiquiu in the Chama Valley, and Nuestra Señora del Rosario, San Fernando y Santiago (Truchas) in 1754. Most of these settlements were on land grants measuring a league (1.61 km) in each cardinal direction from the center of the town, which provided agricultural lands and common grazing and forest lands. In addition to their size, these communities shared other characteristics as a result of their buffer function. Their populations were concentrated in single walled towns built around a central square, or *plaza*. For better defense, adjacent houses had a back wall in common, which formed the outer wall of the settlement. Entrances to the town through this wall, from one to four in number, were no wider than the size of a wagon, and often were defended by a two-story tower, or *torreón*. These buffer towns, to the extent that they followed the prescribed layout, stood in sharp contrast to the dispersed settlement pattern that characterized most eighteenth-century Hispanic communities (Simmons 1969; Swadesh 1974:133–50).

In the event of attack the small garrison of professional soldiers stationed at Santa Fe could not come to the immediate rescue of most settlements. Consequently the buffer towns were required to provide for their own defense. Each settlement had to have a cadre of able-bodied men with mounts and small arms, led by an active member of the militia or a retired army officer. The population of the buffer towns generally included a percentage of those detribalized Indians, famed as frontier fighters, who were known as *Genízaros*.

The *Genízaros* population originated as captives of various tribal origins who were ransomed from nomadic tribes and placed as servants in the homes of settlers and missionaries. Such placement was for the purpose of winning them to the Catholic faith and adapting them to the colonial life-style. By the 1740s, *Genízaros* began to acquire town grants of their own, on condition that they settle athwart the access routes used by nomadic Indians to raid colonial settlements, and that they provide militia service.

In Abiquiu a mission was established for the essentially all-*Genízaro* population, to provide religious and secular education for the "neophytes." In other communities, *Genízaros* constituted a varying percentage of the settlers. They shared the conditions of frontier colonial life, generally existing at the lower end of the economic scale. They were chiefly to be distinguished from other settlers by the disdain inspired by their culturally transitional status. Hence the wry comments on *Genízaros* of various communities written by Fray Francisco Atanasio Domínguez in his 1776 report (Adams and Chavez 1956).

Genízaros as individuals shared with other settlers the chance to improve their fortunes through militia service. Until early in the nineteenth century, for example it was customary for individual militiamen to keep war booty they had seized. Often, this booty included livestock, the effective currency of Colonial times. *Genízaros* also shared in the advantages of trade, most of it contraband, that flourished at some of the buffer communities.

The Tijeras Communities

No permanent settlement in Tijeras Canyon was made in the seventeenth or in the early eighteenth century. At this time the canyon was frequented by Faraon Apaches, who used it as a staging area for raids on the Rio Abajo settlements. We may be reasonably sure, however, that both Indian and Hispanic war and hunting parties, as well as Hispanic woodcutters and prospectors, entered the canyon from time to time, camping there at least for short periods.

By 1763, the Comanche had replaced the Faraon Apache as the most feared, and most admired, of the nomadic raiders of Hispanic hamlets and Pueblo villages. It was in response to this Comanche threat that the land grant called Cañon de Carnue was founded as a buffer community, with its town called San Miguel de Laredo located somewhere within the straggling community now known as Carnuel. On February 6, 1763, when Governor Veles approved the petition for a grant at Carnue, as Tijeras Canyon was then called, he spelled out his objective to "spread the settlements of this kingdom so as to relieve the settlers as the barbaric nations surrounding them are pacified and moved back in accordance with the Royal intention" (NMSRC-NMLG Reel 27, SG 150, Frame 15).

The first Hispanic community of Carnue was the little town of San Miguel de Laredo. The settlement began in 1763 with 17 families, 3 of which were identified as *Genízaros* and 3 as *coyotes*, offspring of European fathers and regional Indian mothers (Swadesh 1976:26–37; NMSRC-SANM II, Reel 10, Frames 405–40). Carnue's designated leader was Second Lieutenant of Milita Cristobal Jaramillo, who, with his brother Juan, probably represented the social and economic apex of Carnue, such as it was. Most of the settlers, like the Jaramillos, came from the Albuquerque area. Soon after its founding the town became a center for trade with friendly Carlana Apaches (Gunnerson 1974:240).

The town was laid out as a square plaza measuring fifty *varas* (some 42.67 m) to a side, around which space was allotted for up to 25 households in the hope of obtaining more recruits for the settlement. Presumably some families lived in cramped quarters while others enjoyed more space. There were some additions to the population in later years, as well as at least one death, that of Juan

Moya the elder, and perhaps some desertions. The entire settlement was abandoned hastily following a Gila Apache raid in October 1770, which resulted in numerous fatalities. The surviving settlers fled to their relatives in Albuquerque. When they refused to resettle and gave up their rights to Carnue, the authorities obliged them in May 1771, to tear down their houses at San Miguel (NMSRC-NMLG Reel 27, SG 150, Frames 7–14).

In 1774, a group of 36 displaced families from the Rio Puerco, including many *Genízaros*, petitioned for the Carnue grant. They were judged to have insufficient arms, mounts, and farm animals to hold the Tijeras Canyon area, and were denied their petition (NMSRC-SANM I, #46).

In 1817, 8 Albuquerque families were permitted to move to San Miguel de Laredo. The following year, two petitions for a formal grant by a total of 47 Albuquerque families, including the 8 resident at San Miguel, were approved. The new Cañon de Carnue Grant was not a town grant but a community grant, with the potential for establishing new villages and hamlets wherever feasible (Figure 27). Its boundaries were apparently the same as those of the original 1763 grant (the documents of which are missing) and the same as the boundaries requested in 1774. The northern boundary was the headwaters of Bear Canyon, north and west of present-day Cañoncito. Another marker for the north boundary was the gypsum cliff which faces Cañoncito from east of present-day State Highway 14. The petitioners wanted land as far north as San Antonito, but they were rebuffed on the grounds that to do this would appropriate privately owned grazing lands shared by livestock owners of the Rio Abajo country (NMSRC-NMLG Reel 27, SG 150, Frame 96).

The south boundary of the grant was Coyote Creek, which runs into Tijeras Arroyo from the southeast, after crossing much of the present-day Sandia Military Reservation. The west boundary was near the entrance to Tijeras Canyon, at a line marked by a tiny rock outcrop called El Huérfano (The Orphan), and the east boundary was the divide east of present-day Sedillo. Claimants of the grant in the 1890s calculated that it contained over 36,000 hectares (Bowden ms. 1969:1725–727).

On February 25 and 26, 1819, Albuquerque Alcade José Mariano de la Peña installed 24 families on the grant at San Miguel de Laredo and 22 families at a settlement called San Antonio de Padua. The San Antonio settlers were given allotments of

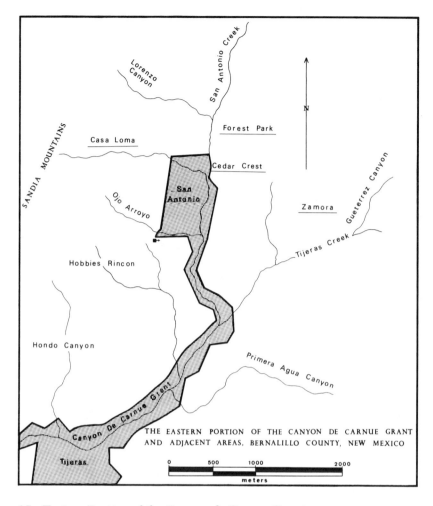

27. Eastern Portion of the Canyon de Carnue Grant.

agricultural land extending southward to the first waterfall on San
Antonio Creek. Subsequent applicants in 1819 and 1820 were installed from below the waterfalls on San Antonio Creek to the
junction with Tijeras Creek, and from there westward to the east
end of present-day Tijeras. Settlers also received lands from the
west end of the grant; principally from the west end of Tijeras to
its center. Most of the canyon from the east end of Carnuel to
Tijeras is too narrow for laying out even the smallest village.

The two towns established in February 1819 were built around
closed plazas, measuring fifty *varas* to a side. It is not clear if the
later 1819 and 1820 settlers were squeezed into these same plazas
or occupied scattered homesteads. The February 1819 settlers
were instructed to have their houses built, their ditches dug, and

their seeds planted by May, and to have their arms and mounts at the ready for militia service. They were also to donate one third of their first two years' harvest to the Royal coffers (NMSRC-NMLG Reel 27, SG 150, Frames 51–56, 94–96, 100–114).

In the early days of the Cañon de Carnue Grant, the settlers had a hard time maintaining a toehold. Repeated Indian attacks forced them to flee and caused many to be reluctant to return. Their reluctance may have had as much to do with recurrent problems of water supply and poor harvests as with the fear of raids. On July 20, 1837, Francisco Ignacio de Madariaga, the legal advisor (*asesor*) of New Mexico, wrote to the New Mexico Departmental Assembly that it was so crucial to maintain an adequate buffer population at San Antonio de Carnue, Las Huertas, and Manzano that it would be advisable to cancel the rights of those settlers who refused to return and assign their allotments to new settlers (NMSRC-SANM I #1148).

From the first year of settlement, the population grew at the northeast end of the grant and dwindled at the southwest end, in part as a result of water problems. It is significant that settlers preferred to live at altitudes where their crops were more subject to late frosts than at Carnuel, where water was insufficient. Tijeras, Cañoncito, and Ranchitos and, especially, San Antonio soon became sizable hamlets although, being deep in the mountains, these communities were more immediately subject to Indian raids than Carnuel.

The economics of the region offer a partial explanation of this seeming paradox. The Cañon de Carnue settlers at most produced subsistence crops, and depended for much of their livelihood on the raising of sheep and goats, using the extensive mountain pasture lands. The men also engaged in mobile occupations, such as cutting wood and carrying it to Albuquerque (Figure 6), buffalo hunting, trading on the plains, and plying the Santa Fe Trail. The opening of mines at the Real de San Francisco del Tuerto (Golden) and, somewhat later, at San Pedro attracted the residents of Tijeras Canyon, first to seasonal prospecting and later to wage work in the mines. When Lieutenant J. W. Abert made his survey in 1846–47, he noticed swarms of prospectors at "Tuerto" (Abert 1962:51).

The impact of male mobility is revealed in Tijeras Canyon oral tradition. The stories relate how when all the men were away, the

women, children, and older people took their pigs and chickens into the houses at the first news of Indians in the vicinity. They
bolted the doors and remained inside until the danger was past.
The Indians in question appear to have been primarily Mescalero
Apaches. There are several early references to the Apache presence
and fear of attack. One documented incident occurred in a later
period, the 1860s, when the Mescaleros had broken out of their
detention at Fort Sumner and struck as far north as Las Vegas and
Galisteo. United States Army troops pursued them and, in their
last desperate resistance, Mescaleros gave or sold two of their own
children to Tijeras Canyon settlers. These children, raised in
Hispanic households, later married into local Hispanic families.

The opening of mines in the area not only provided jobs for
those in Tijeras Canyon but also attracted miners from Mexico
and the United States, some of whom set up at least temporary
residence in Tijeras Canyon communities. The Tijeras Canyon
Census tracts for 1860, 1870, and 1880 show a great deal of
population mobility. Some of the settled families were not present
at the time the census was taken, and other families from elsewhere, many of them transient, were living in the villages. Some of
the newer residents were freighters, who were especially busy
along the Tijeras Canyon route in the 1870s, when they hauled
merchandise to Albuquerque from the railroad terminal at Raton.
Along this route, the round trip by ox-cart took three months.

During the period 1860–80, there had been some population
shifts in the Tijeras Canyon villages. San Antonio, since the mid-
1830s, had been the site of the sole church serving Tijeras Canyon,
since it and nearby Tijeras were the main population centers. In
the census of 1880, Carnuel was listed as having only 10 households, while San Antonio had 35, Tijeras had 15, Cañoncito had
12, Ranchitos had 11, and the newly formed hamlet of Primera
Agua had 9. The southeast end of the grant was also settled as soon
as the Mescalero troubles ended. The new communities were
Cedro, Ojo del Sabino, and Juan Tomás. The communities of
Zamora, Tecolote (Gutiérrez), and Sedillo were also settled near
the east end of the grant.

By the end of the nineteenth century, another church was built
at Santo Niño, the west end of Carnuel. At the east end, the García
family built a private chapel to honor San Miguel de Laredo,
having received from the last family of the generation of 1819 a

bulto (figure in the round) of the patron saint. This *bulto* may have been a community treasure since 1819 or even earlier. Other churches, at Tijeras, Cedro, and Juan Tomás, were built in later years.

Once the nomadic Indians had been forced onto reservations, the Tijeras Canyon communities lost their character as buffer outposts. Because of poor roads through the canyon they continued to be a rather isolated network of villages and hamlets, unified by their common heritage of the land grant and by the dense network of kinship that prevailed among most families. This unity began to erode in the 1890s as a result of two factors. Application to the United States government for confirmation of the land grant had an unsatisfactory outcome, leading to the loss of all but 809 hectares of the original 36,437 hectare grant. The settlers continued to graze on thousands of the remaining acres of the grant for years after the Cibola National Forest had taken over the Carnue grazing and forest lands. The remaining acres of forest land that had been leased were finally closed off altogether at the end of World War II. The grant heirs have had little livestock since that time.

Another factor influencing the erosion of community ties was the drastic change in the economy of the area which began late in the nineteenth century and has continued in the twentieth. When the mining boom and the railway construction era ended, the economy of Tijeras Canyon declined. For a while, the decline was delayed by the opening of coal mines in the area and by the employment of many Tijeras Canyon men in railway construction and maintenance elsewhere in the Southwest. The latter occupation took a number of families out of the canyon for years at a time. The economy experienced a boom during the Prohibition era, when the making of bootleg whiskey for sale in Albuquerque kept a number of families employed. The excellent spring water of San Antonio gave the product a high reputation.

Repeal and the arrival of the Great Depression coincided with a mass return of land grant families to Tijeras Canyon. With no jobs to be had, families returned to subsistence farming, and when possible, the grazing of small herds of livestock. Although some families were able to find work in Albuquerque, the Tijeras Canyon communities had a higher population of subsistence farmers during the decade of the 1930s than at any period since (Figures 28, 29). These circumstances were ended by the outbreak of World War II and a wide dispersion of the population.

28. San Antonio in the early twentieth century. The church, as it was before the fire in 1952, is in the background. The house at the southeast end of the church plaza was built by the Zamora family and was later bought by Maximiano Olguín. He filled in the *zaguán*, a covered coach entry with double doors, here seen as a projecting room.

29. Emilia García de Olguín, a pioneer woman of San Antonio. As a grandmother, she was still a skilled housebuilder.

Even before World War I a new kind of population and economy had entered the Tijeras Canyon area and had begun to displace the older communities and families. The Well Country Ranch near Chanega Springs, a recuperation center for tubercular convalescents, was established, and a growing number of summer vacation homes and resorts began to occupy the hillsides above the villages. The recreation industry with its new population grew at a trickle until U.S. Highway 66 was rebuilt after World War II and a new ski area opened on North Sandia Peak. The remaining lands of the Cañon de Carnue Grant then began to be surrounded by bedroom community developments.

The construction of Interstate Highway 40 has created an even more massive trend toward population growth, changes in land use, and disruption of the land grant villages. Highway 10 and State Highway 14 now literally bisect several of the communities, undermining the integrity of kin, neighbor, social, religious, and economic units.

TECHNOLOGICAL ADAPTATIONS IN TIJERAS CANYON

The early nineteenth-century Hispanic settlers on the Cañon de Carnue Grant were given agricultural allotments in an environment only marginally suited to agriculture. The area is characterized by a semiarid climate, rocky soils, a short growing season, and often, high summer temperatures (Tierney 1976:4). Dendroclimatic studies of 1819–29, the initial settlement period, reveal lower than normal rainfall and above average temperatures. Thus, the first settlers faced climatic conditions harsher than any recorded for recent years.

Climatic studies of the same area from a later period, 1930–39, showed greater than average rainfall and lower than average temperatures, both environmental conditions favorable to agriculture. The same report described farming operations in the local villages as geared solely to subsistence (USDA 1937:15–18) and concluded that dry farming in the area was too great a gamble and that the supply of irrigation water was inadequate.

This environment, unfavorable to either dry or irrigation farming, has nonetheless supported two different societies, each with varying adaptive responses to the same harsh conditions. Some of the social and economic factors that enabled the Hispanic settlers to survive have been explored in the first section of this paper. The technological adaptations were also important.

The differences between Indian and Hispanic technology show up clearly on the ground in the remnants of hydraulic systems. The two water systems tentatively identified as prehistoric Indian systems, were relatively small and simple. Natural floodwater run-off was directed into fields by such water-control devices as rill or arroyo check dams, linear boulder alignments along slope con-tours, and linear rock garden borders (Figure 30). These are

30. Features comprising the San Antonio de Padua Acequia Madre Irri-gation System, Canyon de Carnue Grant.

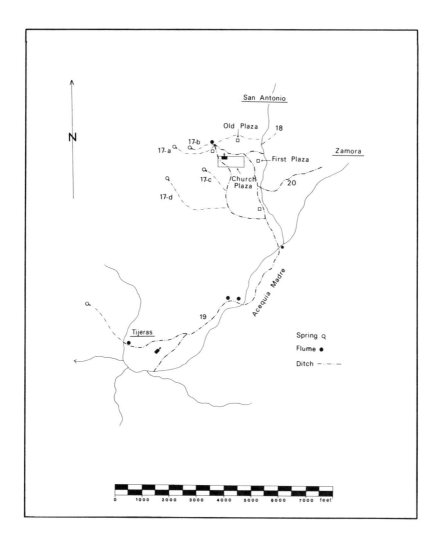

conservation-type systems (Vivian 1974:102) in which water is used in place, and so the land under cultivation must be located at the source of water.

In contrast, the historic systems are more extensive, generally using springs as the primary water source. However, some historic water systems were entirely floodwater fed and others collected floodwater runoff into a spring-fed irrigation network. In the historic period, more elaborate water-control devices, such as irrigation ditches, holding ponds, larger dams, and flumes came into use. These were primarily diversion-type systems (Vivian 1974: 102). In a diversion system, water is moved from its source to wherever it is needed. Thus the amount of cultivated land may be increased, or richer land at a distance from the water source may be used.

The hydraulic systems observed (Figure 30) were either floodwater or spring-fed systems. The dry-farmed fields, which exhibited no hydraulic features other than contour plowing to trap rainfall, were not examined. Table 3 lists the water systems identified in the Tijeras area. Each system on the table is numbered and is referred to in the text by that number. The type of water control device (as near as could be identified) used in each hydraulic system is also listed.

Floodwater Systems

A simple floodwater system employed a crude, temporary pole and brush dam which diverted floodwater from an arroyo into a cornfield. A system like this was observed by Kirk Bryan in 1928 in the Gutiérrez Arroyo channel (system 4). Another, more complex type of floodwater system used water-control devices similar to spring-fed systems, such as ditches and holding tanks, to convey floodwater. The Lorenzo Canyon floodwater system (system 1) is an example. Here, a narrow ditch dug along the base of a steep mountain slope collected and conveyed floodwater runoff to a holding tank, where the water was stored for agricultural use.

These floodwater systems were of a temporary nature because of the unpredictable supply of their source—runoff water. This temporary nature is reflected in the terms *temporal* (seasonal) and *sembrado* (a planting) used by the Spanish-speaking population to distinguish them from fields watered by ditch irrigation, called

TABLE 3. Hydraulic Systems of the San Antonio—Tijeras Region

SYSTEM	SOURCE	TERMINAL	COMPONENTS						USES			PERIODS	
			Ditches	Flumes	Tanks	Dams	Borders	Terraces	Domestic	Agricultural	Industrial	Historic	Prehistoric
1. Lorenzo	Floodwater	Lorenzo Canyon	X		X	X		X		X		X	
2. Casa Loma	Floodwater	Casa Loma Arroyo				X				X		X	
3. Carlito A	Floodwater	Tijeras Village	X	X	X	X	X	X	X	X		X	
4. Gutiérrez A	Floodwater	Gutiérrez Canyon				X	X			X		X	
5. Gutiérrez B	Floodwater	Gutiérrez Canyon	X			X				X		X	
6. Gutiérrez C	Floodwater	Gutiérrez Canyon				?				X		X	
7. Gutiérrez D	Floodwater	Gutiérrez Canyon	X				?			X		X	
8. Sedillo A	Floodwater	Sedillo Locale	?					?		X		X	
9. Sedillo B	Floodwater	Sedillo Locale				X		X		X		X	
10. Zamora A	Floodwater	Zamora Locale	X							X		X	
11. Zamora B	Floodwater	Zamora Locale				X	X	X		X		X	
12. LA 12846	Floodwater	Carnue Locale	?			X		X		X		X	X
13. LA 15961	Floodwater	San Antonio Springs Locale				?		X		X		X	X
14. Tijeras A	Floodwater	Tijeras Locale	?			X				X		X	
15. Tijeras B	Floodwater	Tijeras Locale	?			X		X		X		X	X
16. Primera Agua	Floodwater	Tijeras Locale	X			X				X		X	
17. Acequia Madre	Spring Fed	Tijeras Village	X	X	X		X	X		X	X	X	
18. Initial	Creek Fed	San Antonio	X		?	?			X			X	
19. Tijeras C	Spring Fed	Tijeras Village	X	X	X	X	X	X	X	X	X	X	
20. Zamora C	Spring Fed	Zamora Village	X	X	?	?	X	X	X	X		X	
21. Carlito B	Spring Fed	Tijeras Village	X	X	X	X	X	X	X	X		X	

labor or *labor regado* (Bryan 1929:444). Although the use of these systems in any particular year depended on the amount of seasonal precipitation, they were reused through the years by canyon residents. Some of the floodwater systems may have been prehistoric and were reused by the Hispanic population.

The site designated LA 12846 (system 12) is probably an example of this reuse by later people. It is a simple floodwater system in direct association with a prehistoric, possibly early historic Indian village. The remains consist of three short rock rill dams, two larger rock arroyo check dams, and one earthen arroyo check dam, garden borders, and portions of a basal slope rock alignment. The earthen dam may be of more recent origin than the other features. The system may have been used in this century, as fields are shown in the approximate position of the site on a 1901 surveyor's map of the Cañon de Carnue Grant. The remains of what may be another prehistoric system (LA 15961, system 13), show a simple check dam in association with two one-room structures of prehistoric date located in the San Antonio Springs locale.

Some of the floodwater systems of Hispanic origin were still in use well into this century. Three simple brush and check dam systems, located in Gutiérrez Canyon (systems 4, 5, and 6), were associated with fields that were still producing corn in 1928 (Bryan 1929). The fields associated with the Casa Loma check dam (system 2) were reported as producing only enough crop to yield seed corn in 1931, but in 1932 the yield was fair. Informants state that the dams were located in a small arroyo from which the trapped water was diverted to plots located downstream. This is similar to the system designated Sedillo Locale B (system 9), which was situated at the base of a rocky slope. Runoff was trapped behind a series of short rock contour terraces and diverted to agricultural plots located directly behind the terraces. These plots were planted in the very recent past as evidenced by weathered corn stalks visible in 1975.

Spring-Fed Systems

In April of 1819 Albuquerque Alcalde José Mariano de la Peña sent instructions on the management of irrigation water to the alcalde of San Miguel de Laredo (Carnuel). The instructions stated that an irrigation system was to be completed by planting time, early or mid May, and that the water must be shared among all the settlers. Those who failed to abide by the alcalde's instructions were to lose title to the grant and to be removed (NMSRC-NMLG Reel 27, SG 150, Frame 36). According to la Peña's instructions the irrigation system was to link the settlements of San Antonio, Tijeras, and Carnue through a common water source. The water of San Antonio Creek, which flows into Tijeras Creek at the east end of Tijeras, was to provide the irrigation water.

The first plaza of San Antonio was located on the west bank of the creek. Agricultural allotments were laid out on both banks with the intake of the first system situated on the west bank of the creek just above the first agricultural allotments. Despite the alcade's instructions this first system was abandoned and the location of San Antonio's plaza moved within the first few years of settlement. The quality and quantity of water from San Antonio Creek proved to be inadequate to support an effective hydraulic system.

This Initial System (system 18) (Figure 30) did not draw water directly from springs but from San Antonio Creek, which itself is spring-fed and has a high saline content. The physical remains of the system are scant, consisting of two segments of the same ditch, separated by the Ojo Arroyo near its mouth on the west bank of San Antonio Creek. The first agricultural plot allotted at San Antonio was situated about 420 m north of the rocky hogback known today as La Centinela. About 457 m north of La Centinela is a partially filled-in ditch segment. The ditch runs southward to the Ojo Arroyo. This particular ditch line could easily be all that remains of the first irrigation system, built on orders from Alcalde de la Peña. Although no trace remains of the intake device, it was probably a rock dam placed across the creek and used to divert the water into the ditch. The ditch could carry water to small fields on the north side of the Ojo Arroyo via a *canoa*, a hollowed half-log flume. South of the arroyo, the ditch continued past the Old Plaza and may have continued to Tijeras Village or may have discharged into San Antonio Creek at the first falls.

The settlers replaced the first unsuccessful system with a more elaborate one. The Acequia Madre de San Antonio de Padua (system 17, LA 12847) is the mother-ditch of the San Antonio–Tijeras network of spring-fed hydraulic systems, and the most extensive in the area (Figure 30). It is composed of four interconnecting integral subsystems, two of which also captured floodwater runoff and transported this supplemental water through the ditch network, either directly to agricultural fields or to holding tanks for later use. Each of the subsystems initially took on water from a spring and transported it through a series of ditches, flumes, and holding tanks, some going to locales in the immediate vicinity of each spring for domestic use and for the mills, but most going for agricultural use. The water was then transported by ditches to more distant San Antonio locales for similar use, and from there continued through other ditch networks to the terminal communities of Zamora and Tijeras, where the water discharged into Tijeras Creek. Further downstream, at Carnuel, this water was drawn into other irrigation systems. Some of the known components of the system have been partially obliterated by highway construction and other landscaping activities.

The Acequia Madre of San Antonio, when in full operation, collected water from at least four springs, from San Antonio Creek and from floodwater runoff. It provided water for agricultural and domestic uses and water power for at least two mills built prior to 1850. The Tijeras (system 19) and Zamora (system 20) water works are simple continuations of this larger system.

These ditch systems, constructed with wooden shovels and hoes, required a great deal of ingenuity and village-wide as well as intervillage cooperative effort to build and maintain. The more complex elements undoubtedly were built later than the more elementary ones, but the engineering of each component is impressive. The development of Tijeras Canyon water systems from the simple irrigation of a single field to the elaborate systems serving several communities reflects the technological responses of the populations to the harsh environment.

SUMMARY

The layout of plazas and agricultural allotments supervised by Alcade de la Peña followed San Antonio creek to its confluence with Tijeras Creek, and from there westward toward the narrows of Tijeras Canyon. The waters from these sources were seasonally unreliable and salty, while that from the springs, coupled with floodwater, was of better quality and greater availability. The settlement pattern, then, changed from its original design and spread out as the number of settlers grew and they became more familiar with the characteristics of the land and the climate. The placement of the Hispanic settlements at the east end of the Cañon de Carnue Grant is a reflection of the need to harness water—a resource essential to the survival of these communities.

The Hispanic settlers of Tijeras Canyon were faced with an environment which offered little, but they had the ingenuity which enabled them to survive. To understand why these poeple wanted to settle such an area one must look at the social, economic, and political setting of the late eighteenth century. The principal opportunity for advancement which the colonial empire of Spain could offer to her New Mexican settlers was to place otherwise impoverished people in the ranks of landed gentry (*hidalgos*) by the donation of land grants. Land was then, as it is now, considered one of the most valuable possessions. The colonial government provided the incentive of land ownership to subjects willing to settle in areas which required a defensive position to maintain the safety of the more economically valuable territory. Today the grant heirs in Tijeras Canyon face problems greater than those of their ancestors. The supply of water is still insufficient. The problem has been intensified by the added population and inadequately treated sewage of the bedroom communities above the land grant villages. The response to these contemporary problems will be yet another reflection of the population's adaptation to what is still a harsh environment.

4

Prehistoric Climate
and Agriculture

Linda S. Cordell

EDITOR'S INTRODUCTION

Many reconstructions of southwestern prehistory rely on the notion of climatic deterioration as a motivating factor in cultural change. In order to begin to understand the complex interrelationships between climate and human behavior, it is necessary to establish an accurate reconstruction of the past climate and the range of adaptive strategies open to nonindustrial farmers. In the research at Tijeras, studies of tree-rings provided the basis for inferences about the climate at the time of prehistoric occupation. The alternatives available to the prehistoric farmers are not known in detail; however, the requirements of corn, the technological devices known to have been used by the Anasazi, and data from contemporary southwestern societies provide a framework for inference.

L. S. C.

———————◆———————

Anasazi inhabitants of the Southwest survived by some conbination of agriculture, gathering, and hunting. Although apparently simple, this characterization of the subsistence economy refers to a wide range of complex behaviors. There may have been years or decades when agriculture provided less than one-fourth of the food consumed by a community. At other times, domestic crops made up the major part of the diet. Within the same environment, the kinds of behavior that are most successful for hunters and gatherers can conflict substantially with patterns that are necessary for successful agricultural economies. For example, foragers must be highly mobile in most semiarid inland settings whereas farmers must be sedentary throughout enough of the year to plant, tend, and harvest crops.

Scheduling conflicts of this sort are ameliorated when a group is large enough so that some individuals collect wild foods while others work the land. But if crops are poor year after year, it becomes impossible to support those who are farming, and village abandonment may be necessary. A different problem arises if agriculture is very successful. If farmers are attracted to the area in large numbers and large villages are constructed, then game animals that are wary of man will become scarce. Those animals that are less wary may be hunted to local extinction. In either case, in order to obtain meat, people will either have to travel great distances, or provide agricultural surplus or craft items for trade with groups who are in proximity to game.

Being able to elucidate prehistoric subsistence practices is important to most general theoretical archaeological questions. As noted, the sequence of "events" in Tijeras Canyon is familiar to most of the Anasazi area. There was initial growth of small year-round settlements followed by aggregation into a few communities, and finally by abandonment of these. Two very different explanations for this sequence have been advanced by southwestern archaeologists, although both rely on interpretations of environmental change and subsistence practices.

The older and more traditional explanation assumes that agriculture is nutritionally better or more consistently productive than foraging. Once knowledge of agriculture became available, along with a variety of maize that would grow in the Southwest, people would naturally settle in small villages and become farmers. As people became more familiar with agriculture and better at it, production increased and permitted the formation of large communities. The abandonment of these communities has been ascribed to a number of factors, including disease, warfare, and social strife within villages, but the most common explanation offered for abandonment relates directly to changing climatic conditions, specifically droughts (Douglass 1929; Euler et al. 1979).

More recently, archaeologists have viewed agriculture as a response to local and regional population pressure. The aggregation of people into larger villages is seen as a response to declining crops. It has been suggested that aggregation permits more people to participate efficiently in both production and consumption of food. A larger work force increases the chance of success in bringing in food items from the hunt or from gathering expeditions, and aggregation facilitates the distribution of these items once obtained. If labor intensification is an appropriate strategy to increase yields, aggregation is a way to insure the presence of a large labor force. Finally, aggregation facilitates the exchange of information which can be critical to organizing search efforts for wild food resources or for trade (Martin and Plog 1973; Longacre 1966).

Even in these more recent discussions, abandonment of villages is still generally explained in terms of climatic deterioration, although drought *per se* may not be considered the major factor. Rather, some studies suggest that there may have been a change in the seasonal distribution of rainfall (Schoenwetter and Dittert 1968) or a change in the periodicity of drought years (Jorde 1977). Social factors may also have played an important role in local abandonments, because trade and redistributive networks either broke down or simply were not efficient enough to support many large settlements (Cordell and Plog 1979).

In order to be able to test these two contrasting explanations for the changes in settlement patterns in the Southwest, archaeologists must be able to recover information about the past climate of the area in which they are working, the kinds and abundance of crops people planted, the amounts and kinds of wild plants eaten, and the variety and abundance of game animals hunted. Recently there has been a great effort on the part of a number of specialists to develop methods that are appropriate for reconstructuing the details of past climate in the Southwest (e.g. Euler et al. 1979) There are also new techniques that archaeologists can use to recover information about subsistence resources from the context of sites, some of which are discussed here. Even though we can now provide a considerable amount of detail in discussions of subsistence, we cannot be as precise about minor changes in food resource use as we must be in order to resolve the major theoretical issues.

PALEOENVIRONMENTAL RECONSTRUCTION:
TREE-RINGS

Of the various specialized methods of paleoenvironmental reconstruction available to archaeology, tree-ring studies provide
the most refined results (Euler et al. 1979). All tree-ring studies depend on the fact that certain drought-resistant species of trees, particularly ponderosa pine, Douglas fir, and piñon pine, will produce annular rings of variable width depending upon the amount
of moisture available. Thus, in dry years relatively narrow rings
are formed, and in wet years rings are wider; yet the relationship
between tree-ring width and precipitation is not simple. Ring
width depends on the growth pattern of the particular species of
tree and is affected by general conditions of tree growth. The
width of tree rings, then, depends on the densities of trees in a
forest, soil conditions, and the amount of moisture available as
groundwater. The last may reflect the precipitation pattern of a
number of years. Temperature during the tree's growth period
also influences the width of rings.

The analysis of tree-rings for purposes of extrapolating past
climate depends on a multivariate model of ring growth that was
developed by Harold C. Fritts (1976). Fritts was able to determine
what amount of variation in ring width is directly related to precipitation and temperature. Using his model, it is possible to
estimate prehistoric climate patterns.

A study of tree-rings of piñon pine now growing in Tijeras Canyon was conducted by scientists from the Laboratory of Tree-ring
Research at the University of Arizona (Robinson 1979). The analysis showed that these trees reflect climate in the way Fritts'
(1976) model suggests. Wide rings are produced when moisture
conditions are good during the tree's growth year and when temperatures are cool in early winter, spring, and early summer. With
this relationship established, it was possible for the Laboratory to
extend the tree-ring series back to prehistoric times by using wood
from a number of archaeological sites, including Tijeras Pueblo.
Historic records kept at weather stations over the past fifty years
provide base lines from which the relationship between the deviation of ring width from the mean ring width characteristic of
piñon from Tijeras Canyon can be interpreted to reflect annual
precipitation. The general procedures, which involve a good deal

of statistical manipulation, provide estimated precipitation figures, by year, for the period A.D. 950 and 1970. These estimates are extremely interesting, but as all researchers in paleoclimatic reconstructions agree, they must be interpreted with caution. This is perhaps best demonstrated by comparing the climate data with specific historically documented cases of climate related disturbances.

The historic materials indicate that the Hispanic settlers who moved into Tijeras Canyon in 1819 were to donate one-third of their first two-year's crop to the Royal coffers (Quintana and Kayser, this volume). The accounts also state that there was no crop in the first year (Swadesh 1977). The estimated annual precipitation in Tijeras Canyon, based on tree-rings, for 1819 is 15.49 cm. It is no wonder that the settlers were disappointed by their first year's produce. There are also some documents of serious water shortages that had an effect on the canyon inhabitants which are not reflected in the tree-ring data. For example, Swadesh (1977) indicates that canyon communities suffered in the 1940s, because the springs went dry. The springs occur along geologic contact zones in the Sandia Mountains and are ultimately fed by precipitation. Yet, the tree-ring records for the 1940s do not show unusually low rainfall (as they do for the 1950s), and precipitation in the 1920s and 1930s, which might have had some effect on the springs by the 1940s, was among the most favorable for Tijeras Canyon and for New Mexico as a whole.

Precipitation estimates for the past, derived from tree-rings, are best used as a general guide to climate. The dendroclimatic chart (Figure 31) is intended for this purpose. The "0" line on the chart represents the mean ring width of piñon pine from Tijeras Canyon. The parallel lines above and below the "0" line are drawn to show one and two standard deviations above, and one and two standard deviations below, the mean ring width. The widths of tree-rings from archaeological sites and from living trees for the time span from A.D. 950 to 1970 were measured and each ten-year period averaged. The amount of ring width that correlates consistently with climate has been plotted on the chart by decade, but with a five-year lag. Thus, the first decade is 905–914 and is plotted on the chart at 910. The second decade is 910–919 and is plotted at 915. The resulting curve smooths minor variations and is therefore more likely to be meaningful in terms of climate trends

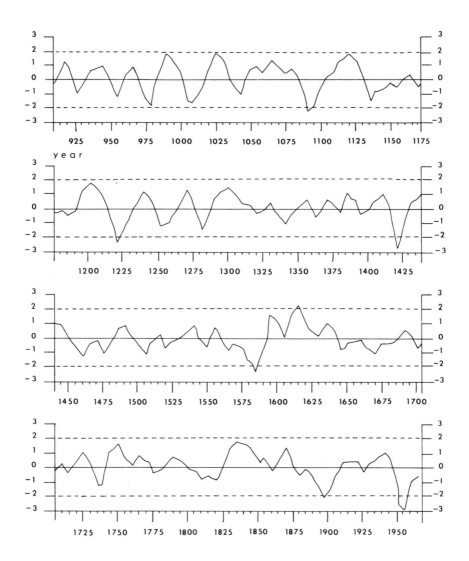

Tree - Ring Chart
Deviation from mean ring width

Normalized decade means overlapped 5 years
910-1965

31. Dendroclimatic chart for Tijeras Canyon based on pinyon pine.

that could have had an effect on prehistoric agricultural practices. In part, this is due to the fact that the ring widths themselves actually reflect available moisture, including groundwater that is retained from precipitation from the previous season. Another reason for using smoothed curves relates to cultural adaptations of agriculturalists. The aboriginal inhabitants of the Southwest, like all subsistence farmers, generally stored the surplus of good years to enable them to survive a few poor years. The results of any one year's crop failure would therefore not result in major behavioral changes such as the abandonment of a community.

The many wood samples (Figure 32) from the early occupation of Tijeras Pueblo indicate that the first large aggregated community at the site was built in A.D. 1313. At that time, the roof timbers for the great kiva were cut, as were construction timbers for many early occupation rooms (Cordell 1977b). Was the population aggregation at Tijeras Pueblo the result of climatic stress as recent theorists suggest? An examination of the tree-ring chart (Figure 31) indicates that precipitation was generally relatively

32. Burned roof support posts were collected to provide a chronology of room construction at Tijeras Pueblo and served for the dendroclimatic reconstruction.

high in the early 1300s, but that it had been low and fairly erratic from about 1225 to 1300. There is certainly no pattern suggestive of a simplistic response to droughts at the time that the pueblo was founded.

Tijeras Pueblo was an active community from A.D. 1313 to about 1425, as suggested by tree-ring dates from the site. The dendroclimatic chart indicates that the entire period was, as a whole, one of the best, in terms of precipitation, in the history of the canyon. As we have noted, the nearly continuous building and refurbishing of rooms at the site was interrupted in the 1360s when about half the original inhabitants seem to have left. The chart shows that precipitation was below normal in the 1340s and in the 1360s, and it is possible that the population decline was a result of these conditions. The 1390s was a period of village renovation, although the site was considerably smaller than it had been. Again, the climate chart indicates that the very end of the fourteenth century was a time of relatively abundant rainfall. Finally, in the early 1400s, the chart shows a rather severe and prolonged period of decreased precipitation.

It is tempting to correlate this with the abandonment of Tijeras Pueblo, but that interpretation may be too simplistic. It seems more likely that the general trend toward drier conditions had the effect of reducing the overall population of the canyon. This is reflected by the decrease in the total number of sites the survey crews located that could be dated to the late fifteenth and sixteenth centuries (Blevins and Joiner 1977). It is possible that because Tijeras Pueblo is in a low canyon setting, and therefore receives less precipitation than higher elevations in the canyon, it was not considered attractive. That Tijeras Pueblo had also declined in population prior to the 1400s may have been important in that the community was no longer a social center or perceived as an auspicious location.

FARMING STRATEGIES

During the 1975 university field season, an elder from one of the Rio Grande pueblos visited Tijeras Pueblo. He remarked that the area appeared to be a very good place to hunt but not a good place to grow corn. His observation is accurate. The area is not heavily farmed today, and only an estimated 30 percent of the land is considered suitable for agriculture with modern farming technology (Naylor 1964:75). In addition to the general problems of short growing seasons and frequently insufficient rainfall, the soils of the canyon are generally clayey or stony, are subject to erosion, and do not make good topsoil (Middle Rio Grande Council of Governments of New Mexico 1974). It is significant that the historic villagers in the canyon supplemented their incomes with timber cutting, mining, and other wage work. The prehistoric inhabitants of the canyon probably used a diversity of agricultural techniques to obtain crops, but they supplemented their diets with wild plant food and with game.

During the excavation of Tijeras Pueblo, numerous charred corn cobs were recovered from rooms and from trash deposits. The corn itself is comparable to that grown at other Anasazi villages. Compared with modern hybrid corn, Pueblo corn is more tolerant of dry conditions. Seeds can be planted very deep in order to tap groundwater, and in dry years the plant will sacrifice height but will produce ears (Castetter and Bell 1942). Prehistoric southwestern farmers cultivated fields with pointed wooden digging sticks, and expended a great deal of effort in maintaining fields. Ethnographic descriptions of agricultural practices among some modern Pueblos record that corn is planted in small artificial hills that are about ten feet apart. As many as 15 seeds are planted in a hole in each small hill (Forde 1931; Titiev 1944). Although the corn plants thus grow in clumps in each hill, this generally protects the inner plant from wind damage and from depredations of field mice and cutworms (Forde 1931; Weatherwax 1954).

Soil and water control features known in the Southwest both prehistorically and ethnographically include irrigation canals, terraces, check dams, bordered fields, and "gravel mulched" gardens (Vivian 1974) (Figure 33). Depending on the topography and soils of an area, these features might occur as single units, or two or more different kinds of features might be integrated into one field system (Vivian 1974). Although ancient fields are not highly visible to the archaeologist, soil and water control features are often encountered and recognized (Woodbury 1961; Vivian 1974).

During surveys in Tijeras Canyon, an intensive effort was made to locate these water control features, but none were found that could unambiguously be dated to the prehistoric period (Cordell

Map of linear borders
and check dams
Point of Pines, Arizona

(Adapted from Woodbury)

contour interval 1 meter

linear border

arroyo

check dam

33. Some of the diverse kinds of prehistoric soil and water control features encountered in the Southwest (after Woodbury).

1977b). The lack of success can be attributed to two factors. First, the relatively good alluvial land in the canyon along the main wash of Tijeras Creek is the most densely inhabited land today, and the most consistently modified by modern road building, quarrying, and other commercial activity. Second, historic soil and water control features are abundant (Quintana and Kayser, this volume), and many of these are probably in the same settings that were used prehistorically. Since local materials were used in both systems, and because the systems themselves involve some of the same technological devices, it is not generally possible to distinguish them.

One important aspect of both the modern and, probably, the prehistoric agricultural systems in Tijeras Canyon relates to questions of general anthropological interest. Some prehistoric southwestern peoples, such as the Hohokam of the Arizona desert (Haury 1976) and the inhabitants of Chaco Canyon, New Mexico (Vivian 1974), relied on very elaborate irrigation features. Today, the Rio Grande pueblos practice irrigation using river water, but the Hopi of Arizona, living in an area devoid of major rivers, disperse their fields in variable topographic situations. A number of theorists argue that complex irrigation systems like those that depend upon rivers require high levels of religious, social, and political control (Wittfogel and Goldfrank 1943). The various water control features discussed by Kayser (Quintana and Kayser, this volume), as well as the remains of isolated, single room prehistoric structures (which may have functioned as field houses) that were noted during the surveys (Blevins and Joiner 1977), suggest that fields in Tijeras Canyon were probably dispersed in a manner more closely resembling Hopi farming practices than those of the modern Rio Grande Pueblos (Cordell 1977a).

5

Analysis of
Plant Remains

Emily Garber

EDITOR'S INTRODUCTION

The foregoing chapters have indicated that farming was not productive or reliable enough fully to support the prehistoric communities in Tijeras Canyon. Garber's paper examines the kinds of wild plant seeds that were found in the archaeological context of Tijeras Pueblo. As her paper cautions, the recovery of seeds from sites does not indicate how, or even if, the plants themselves were used in the past. Her discussion of the uses of these plants among modern southwestern peoples suggests a model for the Tijeras Pueblo population, but there are too many unknown factors in plant use, discard, and preservation to permit further development or testing of such a model.

L. S. C.

American archaeologists have nearly always expressed interest in a variety of environmental data for various reasons. Techniques of extracting such data from local environments of archaeological sites and from the sites themselves, have ranged from the highly subjective look-around-and-get-a-feel-for-the-setting procedures to extremely precise, often standardized schemes.

71

At the Tijeras Canyon archaeological project the interest in environmental data focused on botanical research which began with a survey of current flora in the canyon environs. In 1975 Ann Cully (n.d.), then a graduate student in biology at the University of New Mexico, identified and collected plants from within a transect through a small canyon near Tijeras Pueblo. The transect was selected so that it would include a diversity of exposures and soil conditions. It included a north facing rocky slope, the finer grained and sandy soils of the canyon bottom, and a rocky south facing slope. The plants observed in the general area of the site, as well as those recorded within the transect, are listed in Figure 34.

In many cases, the observed plants in Cully's transect are those that flourish in disturbed ground. Tumbleweed (*Salsola kali*) and summer cypress (*Kochia* sp.) are good examples. The native vegetation in the vicinity of the site has been greatly influenced by road building, foot traffic, archaeology, and other contemporary disturbances. The modern plant profile is, therefore, only a partial reflection of prehistoric conditions in the area. Since all plants utilized by prehistoric inhabitants may not have occurred in the immediate vicinity of the site, modern plant lists are a poor scale with which to determine what plants were used by the Tijeras peoples. In order to supplement Cully's data, this research focused on analysis of botanical specimens excavated from the Tijeras site. These are listed in Table 4.

During the excavation of Tijeras Pueblo, various samples of plant remains were taken for later analysis (Figure 34). The samples consisted of soils taken from features such as cists, hearths, and bins, from stratigraphic columns, burials, and trash deposits. These were subjected to flotation, a relatively new but fairly common procedure, in order to extract small seeds and bits of plant material.

The flotation itself involves an often makeshift apparatus of household equipment. Techniques vary slightly from analyst to analyst, but most use some method to maximize the material recovered. For the Tijeras material, we used the following system. The soil from each sample was placed in the innermost of two nested buckets. Water was run into the inner bucket so that seeds, charcoal, and any other nonsoil material would float to the top. The inner bucket was allowed to overflow, and the floating material was carried into the outer bucket. The water in the outer bucket was then strained through chiffon.

TABLE 4. Plants Excavated from Tijeras Pueblo

	Excavated From Trash Area	Excavated From Room Area
Zea mays (corn)	X	
Nicotiana sp. (tobacco)		
N. attenuata	X	X
N. trigonophylla		
Chenopodium sp. (goosefoot)	X	X
C. berlandieri	X	
C. dessucatum	X	X
C. fremontii	X	
C. incanum		X
C. Watsonii	X	X
Portulaca retusa (purslane)		X
Polanisia trachysperma (clammyweed)	X	
Solanum jamesii-douglasii (nightshade)	X	
Juniperus scopulorum (Rocky Mountain juniper)	X	
Echinocereus sp. (strawberry cactus)	X	
Sporobollus sp. (dropseed)	X	
Sprorbollus contractus (spike dropseed)	X	
Cruciferae sp. (mustard family)	X	
Graminae sp. (grass family)	X	
Physalis hederofolia-foetens (ground cherry)	X	
Tidestromia ? (amaranth family)	X	
Polygonaceae (buckwheat family)	X	
Malvaceae ? (mallow family)	X	
compositae (astor family)	X	
Amaranthus (pigweed)	X	
Cleome serrulata (Rocky Mountain bee plant)	X	
Nut fragment	X	

When the material in the chiffon dried, it was placed under a binocular microscope for inspection. Seeds are often much smaller than one would expect. Corn and sunflower seeds, for instance, are veritable giants in the seed world. During the flotation process, it may appear that nothing is floating out of the soil. Closer inspection reveals specks that may be identified as seeds under the microscope. Taxonomic work then begins. Seeds may be classified sometimes as closely as species. In this way, an analyst may generate a list of seeds found in each separately inspected sample. In addition to seeds, our emphasis here, bits of wood in the form of charcoal may be seen, as may small snails and parts of insects.

Although the identification of seeds is time-consuming and tedious, interpretation is far more difficult. The presence of a seed in a sample may reflect many things. Ethnographic sources, for example, report that wild weed plants are often allowed free reign

Pinus edulis	Pinyon pine
Juniperus scopulorum	Rocky Mountain juniper
Juniperus monosperma	one-seeded juniper
Agropyron sp.	wheat grass
Bouteloua gracilis	blue grama
Bouteloua curtipendula	side oats grama
Polypogon monospeliensis	rabbit foot grass
Stipa comata	needle and thread grass
Poa sp.	blue grass
Yucca bacata	yucca
Yucca angustissima	narrowleaf yucca
Populus sp.	cottonwood
Quercus grisea	gray oak
Atriplex canescens	four wing salt bush
Eurotia lanata	winter fat
Salsola kali	tumbleweed
Kochia sp.	summer cypress
Lesquerella sp.	bladderpod
Lepidium sp.	
Cercocarpus montanus	mountain mahogany
Petalostemum canidum	prairie clover
Psorlea sp.	scurf pea
Melilotus sp.	sweet clover
Croton texensis	dove weed
Opuntia sp.	prickly pear
Mammilaria sp.	pincushion cactus
Asclepias speciosa	milkweed
Verbena pinnatfida	verbena
Cucurbita feotedissima	stinking gourd
Cirsium sp.	thistle
Chrysothamnus nauseosus	rabbit bush
Ratibida tagetes	prairie cone flower
Gutierrezia sp.	snakeweed

34. List of plants found growing in the vicinity of Tijeras Pueblo, identified by A. Cully.

on trash middens. Thus, plants that enjoy disturbed soil may thrive on a site despite the fact that they were used infrequently or not at all by the inhabitants of the site. Even if we limit ourselves to samples taken from prehistoric rooms, there are risks in interpretation. Seeds, beings as small as they are, may be brought into a room by a number of means. They may stick to clothing as one goes through a field, or they may have been picked up accidentally when a gatherer was collecting a different plant. One interesting study conducted at a site in Chaco Canyon, New Mexico, showed that two samples, one of seeds and the other of pollen, taken from the same place on the floor of the same room resulted in very different plant lists (Cully 1979; Struever 1977). Thus, it is not at all clear precisely how the presence of seeds in an archaeological site reflects human behavior.

There are additional difficulties of differential preservation as a result of prehistoric food-processing techniques, fungi in the soil, acidity, differences in seed maturity within a species that may affect preservation, and probably a host of other problems that we have yet to contemplate. Until the processes that affect seed preservation are better understood, perhaps through some controlled experimentation, discussions of plant remains are tenuous at best. The absence of plant species or genera does not indicate the absence of that species during prehistoric times. The frequency of particular seed types compared to others does not necessarily reflect the frequency or proportion of that seed as a food source in the diet. Also, in dealing with seed or plant remains, it is important to remember that what is found intact is most often a reflection of what was not consumed or used.

Reported ethnographic uses of plants demonstrate that members of non-industrial societies have a sophisticated knowledge of their environment. The prehistoric inhabitants of Tijeras Canyon must have known which plants are edible, when and where they are found, and how to prepare them. As interpretation of archaeologically excavated plant remains is difficult, ethnographic descriptions provide a partial model of the uses of the various plants recovered.

The seeds discussed here were identified in samples taken from features at Tijeras Pueblo. These features included hearths and mealing bins that we hope could be more clearly related to the human activities at the site. The most interesting, and apparently controversial, seeds recovered were those of *Nicotiana attenuata* and *Nicotiana trigonophylla*—tobacco.

TOBACCO (*NICOTIANA ATTENUATA* AND *N. TRIGONOPHYLLA*)

Tobacco use by American Indians and, more specifically, southwestern Indians has been widely recorded by anthropologists. The

Hopi, among others, have been known to cultivate tobacco from time to time (Whiting 1966:90), but the plant, which enjoys disturbed areas, may have flourished with little or no human intervention on pueblo trash mounds. The Zuni (Stevenson 1915), the Hopi, the Navajo (Elmore 1944:75), and a number of the Rio Grande pueblos (Robbins, Harrington, and Freire-Marreco 1916: 103) among others, used tobacco for ceremonial and medicinal purposes. At San Ildefonso Pueblo, tobacco was reportedly used medicinally to cure toothaches. The people of Santa Clara reportedly believed that the plant, when used as snuff, could stop nose discharges or, when placed on the neck, could cure coughs. Tobacco mixed with *Gutierrexia longifolia* (snakeweed) and *Artemesia* (sagebrush) was given as snuff to women in labor (Robbins et al. 1916:106).

While many archaeologists have assumed that tobacco use was also prevalent in prehistoric times, there is actually little archaeological evidence for this assumption (Castetter 1943; Switzer 1969). Tobacco is rare in the archaeological record. A few species have been identified in sites in Arizona and New Mexico. These specimens, however, were discovered in unusual contexts of extremely fine preservation; inside ceramic vessels and in a number of cave sites (Switzer 1969:13). All these finds were of leafy plant parts. Few people have discussed tobacco seed remains. It stands to reason that when one smokes tobacco leaves, little will remain for the archaeologist but ashes. Consequently, finds of tobacco leaves will be extremely rare. But, if seeds were separated from the leaves prior to use, we might expect to find uncarbonized seed remains. (None of the tobacco seeds at Tijeras showed any evidence of burning.)

Why, then, have we little evidence of tobacco in seed form in the archaeological record? This author believes it is primarily because archaeologists have been generally ill-informed as to the size of most seeds. Many people use window screen as the smallest sifter in the flotation procedure. For example, archaeologists at one site in Arizona sifted flotations through a 1.8 mm mesh screen. Prior to the arrival of the paleoethnobotanist, any material smaller than the mesh was discarded as detritus (Bohrer 1970:413). *Nicotiana attenuata* and *N. trigonophylla* seeds average 0.6 to 1.0 mm in their greatest dimension (Knight 1978:142). While quite a few other seeds of larger size were recovered, it seems reasonable to

assume that if there were any *Nicotiana* seeds (or any others in
that size range) at this Arizona site, they would have been lost with
the "detritus" (Figure 35). In the next few years, however, with
more basic botanical knowledge filtering into the discipline (e.g.
Bohrer and Adams 1977; Knight 1978; Minnis and LeBlanc
1976), we should see these mistakes eliminated. We might also see
many more tobacco seeds in our sites!

Tobacco still occurs in or near the Tijeras Canyon area, and
since the seeds occur with great (and in some cases surprising) frequency in some of the samples examined, it is quite possible that
the plant was aided in some way by the prehistoric Indians
(Knight, personal communication 1978). Historically, southwestern Indians did not cultivate tobacco with the same care as they
would food crops. Sometimes the plants were aided in their
growth by the burning of areas where the plants would then thrive
on the disturbed plots. At times Indians reportedly spread tobacco
seed on the ground to foster the germination of a crop in the loca-

35. Wild tobacco (*Nicotiana*) and maize seeds drawn to scale.

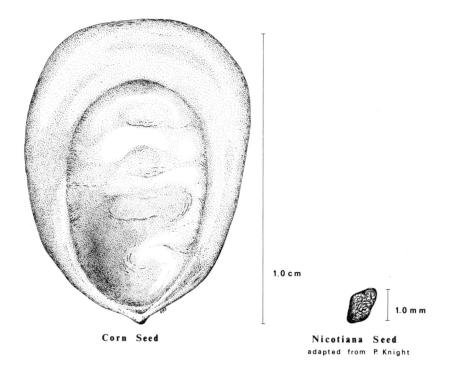

1.0 cm

1.0 mm

Corn Seed

Nicotiana Seed
adapted from P. Knight

tion of their choice. Whatever the behavioral context of these plant remains, their appearance in the record is provocative in itself.

CORN (*ZEA MAYS*)

Corn is undoubtedly the most important agricultural plant found in the archaeological record of the North American Southwest. It occurs often in flotation samples and is frequently recovered during excavation in the form of cobs and kernels. More often than not, it is carbonized, having been burnt. Most of the corn remains in the Tijeras flotation samples were burnt fragments of kernels. One sample examined, taken from the underside of a metate (a grinding stone) in room 92 (Figure 36) revealed what may be uncarbonized ground corn remains.

The many uses of corn as a staple among the Indians of the Southwest is well known and will not be dealt with extensively here. Historically, the Tewa planted their corn in April and

36. Some room floors at Tijeras Pueblo yielded a number of grinding implements. Flotation samples were taken from metates (upper right), hearths, and ashpits (center).

gathered it in late September and early October. After the harvest the entire community spent several days husking corn and storing it (Robbins, Harrington, and Freire-Marreco 1916:82). Suffice it to say that corn played a large part in the subsistence of prehistoric Southwesterners.

GOOSEFOOT (*CHENOPODIUM* SPECIES)

It is not unusual to find ample representation of *Chenopodium* species (Figure 37) at archaeological sites in the Southwest (Knight 1978:84). Many species of this plant were used historically and prehistorically. The Zuni report that these plants are among the most important of their food plants (Castetter 1935:21 and Stevenson 1915:66). Certainly *Chenopodium* are of multiple use.

The Acoma, Laguna, Hopi, Zuni, Jemez, most of the Rio Grande Pueblo peoples, Spanish Americans, Mescalero Apache (Castetter 1935:16), Cochiti (Lange 1959:149), Zia (White 1960: 560), and the Navajo (Elmore 1944:43–44), among others, have eaten the greens raw or boiled them with fat or meat for consumption. The plants are usually used for their greens when they are quite young. The Acoma and Laguna report having dried the greens for winter use (Castetter 1935:16). Among the Navajo, finely chopped greens were used as an insect repellent. When spread on the face and arms *Chenopodium* is said to keep flies and mosquitoes away. The Navajo also report that the plant is "like soap when crushed" (Elmore 1944:44).

The seeds of *Chenopodium* plants also served as important sources of food. They were used in the same manner as corn. Tortillas and bread were made by numerous Southwestern groups after parching and grinding the seeds (Castetter 1935:23; Elmore 1944:44; Lange 1959:149). The Zuni prepared pats or balls from a mixture of ground *Chenopodium* seed, corn meal, salt, and water and steamed them for food (Castetter 1935:21). In a rather interesting use, the Navajo obtained sugar by chewing parched *Chenopodium* seed meal (Castetter 1935:23; Elmore 1944:44).

All the *Chenopodium* species found at the site could have occurred naturally in the Tijeras locality in prehistoric times. In New Mexico *Chenopodium berlandieri* and *C. dessicatum* occur in waste ground areas between 4,500 and 8,000 feet elevation. *C. incanum* is found at elevations of 3,500 to 6,500 feet on dry plains

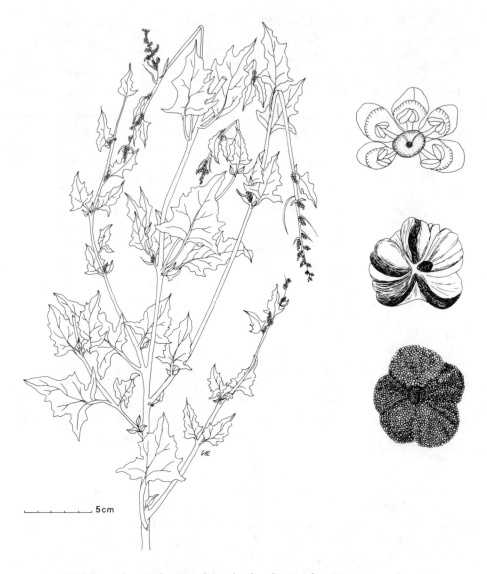

37. Goosefoot (*Chenopodium berlandieri*) (after Matsumura).

and hills, and *C. watsonii* occurs on dry plains between 5,000 and
7,000 feet. *C. watsonii* and *C. incanum* fruit and form mature
seeds between June and October. *C. dessicatum* goes into fruit between July and November, and *C. berlandieri* fruits between
August and November (Knight 1978).

These specifications would undoubtably vary slightly according
to elevation and other local environmental factors, but if need be,

the prehistoric inhabitants of Tijeras Pueblo could have gathered greens early in the summer months or late spring. Seeds from these plants would have been available over a wide range of time (probably, in some years, before, during, and after the corn harvest). If greens were used by the prehistoric inhabitants of Tijeras Pueblo when the plants were young, we would not expect to find archaeological remains of the food processing in the guise of mature seeds. Thus, our evidence of *Chenopodium* use is biased in favor of plant-gathering activities during those months when the plants were in seed.

Chenopodium seeds were found in both the trash deposits and the features at Tijeras. *C. watsonii*, *C. incanum*, and *C. dessicatum* were all found in the sample taken from the bottom of the metate in room 92. All were in perfect condition, showing no obvious signs of grinding, although they were carbonized, perhaps indicating parching. *Chenopodium* was also found in the hearth samples examined. It must be remembered, however, that these seeds are minute (averaging about a millimeter in size) and could easily be lost in a room.

PURSLANE (*PORTULACA RETUSA*)

Portulaca retusa (Figure 38) was defined in a number of contexts in the pueblo. Along with the *Chenopodium* species and *Nicotiana attenuata*, it was found under the metate in room 92, as well as in the trash deposits. *Portulaca retusa*, like the *Chenopodium* species, occurs well within the range of Tijeras Pueblo and would have been easily accessible. It grows in waste areas of sandy or saline soils at elevations between 4,000 and 7,500 feet and probably occurs in many locations in the canyon. The fruit of the plant matures from August through November (Knight 1978:119).

Purslane has been widely used by the Southwestern Indians. The Tewa added the finely chopped plant to gravy (Robbins et al. 1916:61). At Isleta the people would gather large quantities of the plant and then dry it slowly in an oven so that it might be stored as greens for the winter (Castetter 1935:43). Among the Acoma and Laguna, purslane was cooked with meat and eaten much as we eat spinach. Most of the New Mexico Pueblos boiled the plant for food (Castetter 1935:43; Swank 1932; Lange 1959:150).

Purslane's medicinal uses were varied. The Navajo ate purslane

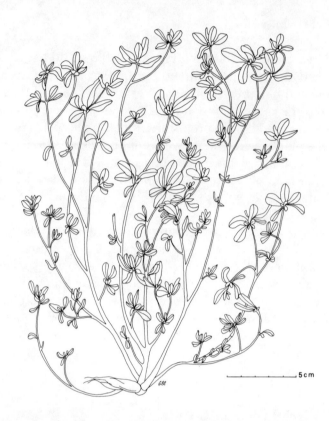

38. Purslane (*Portulaca retusa*) (after Matsumura).

as a cure for stomach aches (Elmore 1944:47). At Acoma and Laguna a tea would be brewed as a cure for diarrhea and as an antiseptic to reduce blood clots (Swank 1932:62 and Castetter 1935:43). The plant was primarily, then, utilized for its greens and not for its seeds.

CLAMMY WEED (*POLANISIA TRACHYSPERMA*)

This plant occurred only once, in a sample taken from the trash deposits. Ethnohistorically, clammy weed was used much as was Rocky Mountain Bee Plant (*Cleome serrulata*) (Figure 39) and, in fact, was considered to be the same plant by the Acoma and Laguna. Among these peoples the plants were used for their greens and seeds. The seeds were gathered in the fall and then dried on willow sticks; in winter they were cooked into mush (Swank 1932: 62; Castetter 1935:25). The Tewa of Hano and the Hopi gathered

39. Rocky Mountain bee plant (*Cleome serrulata*) (after Matsumura).

Rocky Mountain Bee Plant in midsummer and then boiled it for a long time to counteract its very alkaline taste. The Tewa boiled the plant into a thick, black mixture which was then poured onto boards to dry and harden into cakes. The cakes were soaked in hot water and then fried in grease (Castetter 1935:24).

A number of Pueblos made use of *Polanisia trachysperma* and *Cleome serrulata* as a source of paint for decorating pottery (Lange 1959:147; Robbins et al. 1916:61), and it is believed that some carbon black paint on prehistoric pottery in the Southwest was derived from these plants.

The plants also had a number of ceremonial uses. At the end of one Zuni ceremony, *Opuntia* (prickly pear cactus) and willow switches were used to whip the participants, then *Polanisia* root and blossoms were chewed and ejected all over their bodies (Stevenson 1915:96).

Polanisia trachysperma is usually found in sandy stream beds at an elevation between 4,000 and 7,000 feet. It fruits between June and November.

WILD POTATO (*SOLANUM JAMESII-DOUGLASII*)

The seeds of *Solanum jamesii* and *S. douglasii* (Figure 40) are apparently indistinguishable (Knight 1978:132). The specimens found at Tijeras Pueblo came from two different areas of the trash deposit.

The tubers of these plants, which are about the size of a cherry, were used for their food value by a number of the New Mexico Pueblos (Swank 1932:70). The Hopi boiled the tubers and ate them with a greasy talc called potato clay (Castetter 1935:51). *Salanum jamesii* tubers were eaten raw, boiled, or baked by the Navajo. Alum was sometimes added to prevent vomiting (Elmore 1944:75). The Apache reportedly gathered *S. jamesii* in August and boiled them unpeeled. The tubers were sometimes dried and stored and later ground into flour for bread (Castetter and Opler 1936:42).

ROCKY MOUNTAIN JUNIPER
(*JUNIPERUS SCOPULORUM*)

One badly burned juniper berry was discovered in a sample that had been contaminated by twentieth-century archaeologists. Juni-

5 cm

40. Wild Potato (*Solanum jamesii*) (after Matsumura).

per berries are apparently a good food source, and were eaten either raw or stewed (Cook 1930:24). The trees are found between elevations of 7,000 and 8,500 feet in the Sandia Mountains (Martin and Hutchins 1975:23.

STRAWBERRY OR HEDGEHOG CACTUS (*ECHINOCEREUS*)

Echinocereus seeds are indistinguishable at the species level (Knight 1978:37). Thus, we have no hint at which of the *Echinocereus* cacti the seed found in the trash represents.

The fruit of this plant, called tunas, was eaten by many of the Pueblo peoples (Swank 1932:42; Castetter 1935:26). The seeds of this genus are small enough (.8–1.5 mm.) to be eaten along with the fruit (Knight 1978:37). The pulp of the fruits was prepared in a number of ways; it was sliced and baked as squash, made into a sweet pickle by baking with sugar, made into candy, or macerated and made into a cake cooked with sugar. The Cochiti roasted the stems in a dugout pit prior to consumption (Castetter 1935:26).

DROP-SEED GRASS (*SPOROBULUS CONTRACTUS*)

A few *Sporobolus* seeds were found in trash samples. In a number of cases the species could not be determined. Those that were identifiable at the species level were *S. contractus.*

Sporobolus contractus occurs on dry mesas, bluffs, and sand hills between 3,000 and 6,000 feet. It bears fruit from late August through November (Knight 1978:107). The Hopi ground drop-seed grass with corn meal for food. Dumplings, rolls, and griddle cakes were cooked by the Navajo from ground drop-seed (Castetter 1935:28).

SUMMARY

The seeds recovered during excavation at Tijeras Pueblo reflect the wide range of plant life available to the inhabitants. If used in manners similar to those recorded for the southwestern ethnographic cases, many of these plants could have provided substantial food sources either consumed fresh or dried for future use. It may be that our fascination with agricultural strategies has tended to obscure the obvious importance of wild food resources.

This article has demonstrated that archaeology is, in some cases, very far from its stated goals. This is fine as long as we know the pitfalls and learn to work around them and with them. Knowing the historic uses of plants in itself will probably not aid us in understanding everything about why people change their cultural adaptations. It does tell us, however, that there may be some similarities between the past and the present in terms of how people go about organizing their work for survival.

Two things are of pressing importance for any future study. First, we must be able to understand the problems and possible solutions facing peoples living in environmental settings similar to that of Tijeras Pueblo (see Anderson and Oakes, this volume). Second, we cannot discuss change at a particular site unless we have an idea of what that behavioral change would look like in the archaeological remains available to us. We must begin some controlled experimentation with plant parts. Without an understanding of why some plants survive archaeologically and others do not, we will never be able to be certain of any of our ideas about the archaeological remains.

ACKNOWLEDGMENTS

A number of people have served very important functions during this research. Without the patience, teaching, and friendship of Paul J. Knight the research probably never would have been undertaken. Paul was kind enough to lend me his time and to allow me to use his M.A. thesis as a key for typing the seeds. We held numerous discussions on the subject of paleoethnobotany and I'm sure that many of the ideas presented in the following pages were derived from our discussions. Dr. Linda S. Cordell granted her confidence and procured funds for the support of this project. She proved to be very understanding and helpful as my notions about paleoethnobotany jelled. Rod Harada and Jean Williams worked tirelessly floating material and sorting seeds from other debris in the samples. Christina G. Allen helped set up the laboratory prior to my arrival on the scene. And Carrie Strom lent me an evening during which we floated quite a few samples. All of these people were generous with their time and their thoughts. I thank them very much.

6

Analysis of
Faunal Remains

Gwen Young

EDITOR'S INTRODUCTION

As Young's paper indicates, the analysis of faunal remains from archaeological contexts is further advanced than that of seed remains. Young develops models of the prehistoric hunting and meat processing activities that may have been pursued in Tijeras Canyon. She is able to evaluate her models using data from Coconito, Tijeras Pueblo, and San Antonio and to compare these sites with respect to meat procurement, butchering, and cooking. Although she finds no evidence of scarcity of meat at the sites, the degree to which animal bones were processed suggests that some segments of the prehistoric population may have suffered nutritional deficiencies.

L. S. C.

As archaeological concern shifts toward understanding the lifestyles of prehistoric groups, there is a growing interest in delimiting the food-getting behavior of archaeologically known peoples. The ways in which groups coped with changes in the availability of foods they depended on, and how this in turn affected their social relations with other groups, have become major interests. Simple lists of the animals found in trash middens no longer suffice to answer the questions about nutrition and economic patterns that archaeologists ask.

The concern with more thoroughly examining and interpreting animal remains derives from the interests of two groups of archaeologists. Those archaeologists dealing with the remains of Paleo-Indians and Archaic hunter-gatherer groups became interested in the season of year of kills and the implications of remains for interpreting butchering practices. The studies of huge bison drives in the western United States by Kehoe and Kehoe (1960) and White (1954) exemplify this. European researchers, investigating the origins of animal domestication, provided a series of in-depth analyses of the morphology of bones of particular species and of the initial uses of domesticated animals (see Angress and Reed 1962).

The trend to more detailed forms of faunal examination failed to stimulate New World researchers studying the remains of agriculturalists lacking animal husbandry, such as the Pueblo groups of the Southwest or prehistoric groups of the Mississippi drainage (Davis 1960). Agriculture was thought to have obviated the need for any substantial reliance on hunting. Hunting was viewed as a casual occupation infrequently engaged in, and certainly not necessary for the survival of any agricultural community. These assumptions were based on what we now consider very scanty evidence. Unfortunately, they have been accepted as "truths" until very recently.

Such assumptions may have been plausible in areas outside the semiarid Southwest—areas where environmental conditions were more favorable for assuring high agricultural yields. In Tijeras Canyon, as in most of the mountain and desert regions of New Mexico and Arizona, the combination of two variable and unpredictable factors—the amount and distribution of rainfall, and the length of the growing season—would have made total dependence on corn and beans a very hazardous means of subsistence. Even present inhabitants of Tijeras Canyon, armed with modern technological equipment such as power tools, chemical fertilizers, and with the advantages of modern storage processes, cannot subsist on the meager returns of their produce for any significant period of consecutive years. It seems obvious, then, that hunting must have retained an important position in the prehistoric com-

munities. It would have acted as a buffer mechanism, or safe-
guard, against fluctuations in agricultural yields.

A look at human dietary requirements suggests another reason
for considering the importance of animal resources among prehistoric agriculturalists. Corn provides a less than adequate portion
of protein for any individual. Only 3.5 grams of protein are available per 100 grams (3.5 oz) of corn (the equivalent of a 10.16 cm.
cob), as opposed to 21 grams of protein for an equivalent amount
of venison or wild rabbit (Agricultural Research Service 1963).
The average daily protein requirement for persons age eleven or
older ranges from 44 to 56 grams (Kirschmann 1975:237); hence,
each individual would have to consume at least 15 cobs of corn
per day for adequate protein. Beans contain about the same
amount of protein per unit of weight as meat, but they lack certain
amino acids necessary for protein synthesis within the body. Meat
may also have been important to insure an adequate intake of iron
in the prehistoric diet. Iron of animal origin is better absorbed
than a comparable amount from vegetable sources, because it contains certain amino acid "enhancers" (Layrisse 1969). Lack of
supplemental animal protein could result in possibly fatal iron-
deficiency anemia (see Ferguson, this volume). Hunting, then,
would be essential to agriculturists for the protein and amino acids
it supplies.

Ideally, we would like to be able to measure the relative degree
of dependence on agriculture as compared to hunting, in order
better to understand exactly how hunting acted as a resource buffer. At our present level of methodological sophistication this is
not possible. We can, however, measure the relative importance of
the different animal species exploited, the degree to which each
was utilized, and the implied extent of intercommunity effort involved in hunting, butchering, and distributing the kill. Based on
on certain assumptions, this information can be used to infer
possible periods of relative stress when the agricultural yields over
time may have been less than sufficient to sustain the inhabitants
of the canyon. The purpose of this paper is to explore these particular questions using the data from samples of three excavated prehistoric communities in Tijeras Canyon—Coconito, San Antonio,
and Tijeras Pueblo.

Our present understanding of the temporal relationships among
these three sites has been discussed (Chapter 1). For the purpose of

this analysis, the temporal relationships among the various occupations and the terminology used in this chapter are clarified a bit further. The "time-line" in Figure 41 illustrates what we now believe to be the approximate span of each occupation, based on available tree-ring dates and ceramic analyses (see Phillips, this volume). The labels for each period correspond to those used in previous publications. The dates for Coconito and Tijeras Pueblo site periods are the best documented, while those for the San Antonio site are, at this point, less well defined. Breaks in the lines of a site indicate probable abandonments of the site (see Phillips, this volume). Divisions in a continuous line, such as between the Middle and late Middle San Antonio periods, indicate a finer temporal division within a single, continuous occupation.

It was impossible to examine all the faunal remains from the excavated portions of the sites for this report. The samples of each site used here are primarily from areas where remains had been previously identified by other researchers and myself before the conception of this book (Nelson 1978; Teglia 1977; Young 1978; and Jill Mc Gowan, Henry Mesing, and Lynn E. Cunningham). Additional identifications were made of remains from areas needed to round out the types and locations of areas already

41. Time line of occupations compared in faunal analysis.

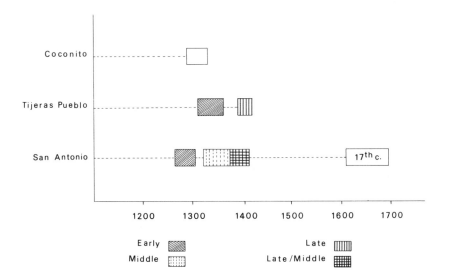

sampled. The additional areas included larger trash middens and, where possible, a sample of rooms for each occupation.

Certain problems inherent in using these samples should be mentioned, because they may bias the results. First, the sizes of the samples from each site and period vary, as do the proportions of total area of each site sampled. The ratio of rooms examined to trash deposits examined also varies among sites and periods. The ratio of identifiable to unidentifiable fragments varies among sites, reflecting, in part, the abilities of individuals doing identification rather than the nature of the remains. Such problems should not, and have not, been dismissed. Attempts were made to evaluate the effects of each of these problems in the following analyses and some are discussed in the final section of the paper. In instances where some bias was suspected, or where evaluation of the effects of these and other problems were impossible, less emphasis is given the results.

One problem, not related to sampling, cannot be evaluated: the differential recovery of animal remains during field excavations. Attempts were made, of course, to recover all animal bones, using the techniques used to recover artifactual materials—sifting excavated dirt through small-meshed screens (Figure 42). The bones of very small animals and birds, as well as tiny bone fragments, could conceivably have slipped through the screens. Parts of such animals, then, may be underrepresented in the remains. The bias is probably minimal, but possible excavation error should be acknowledged. Again, results that may have been conditioned by differential recovery have been de-emphasized.

ASSUMPTIONS AND EXPECTATIONS

It is frequently useful for anthropologists, economists, cultural geographers, and other social scientists to assume that people will expend as little effort as possible in attempting to obtain sufficient resources. The utility of assuming that the "law of minimum effort" applies to food procurement activities is that it enables us to predict expected behavior, with which actual behavior may be compared (see Jochim 1976 for discussion of this approach in general and its application to hunting and gathering).

In our daily lives, we may measure the effort or "cost" of doing a particular errand by weighing, often unconsciously, the benefit

42. Screening dirt. All excavated earth was screened through one-quarter-inch mesh.

of the "return" gained from the product of the errand against its cost in terms of physical effort and, most likely, the amount of gasoline (another form of energy) expended.

In studying preindustrial societies, cost can be estimated in terms of the amount of time and effort spent in procuring food and in the distance traveled to obtain it. Research among groups such as the !Kung Bushmen of Africa (Lee 1969) has attempted to measure this cost directly by calculating the energy, measured in calories, obtained from resources against the amount of calories expended to acquire them. Such a unit of measure can then be used to compare the strategies of one group to those of others in a given region (see the series of articles by Cook, Kemp, and Rappaport, *Scientific American* 1971).

Archaeologists, of course, cannot go back in time and observe the people of Tijeras Canyon to measure the costs of hunting in any one period nor to observe any changes through time. Hunting may have become more labor-demanding in response to factors such as population growth or environmental change, or conversely, have required less time and energy, because of improved conditions. We can, however, state what we do know about the economy and how we would expect the groups to behave under optimal conditions of resource availability and under conditions of resource deficiencies. We know that by A.D. 1300 they were sedentary agriculturalists supplementing and, we assume, buffering their diet by hunting. They would have attempted to get the most from their resources while spending the least effort, but in such a way that hunting would not interfere with the demands of practicing agriculture.

With optimal conditions we would expect people to (1) maximize the amount of meat gained per unit of effort expended in hunting; (2) minimize the time taken to locate game; (3) minimize the distance traveled to hunt; (4) maximize the likelihood of capturing something for the effort; (5) adopt a seasonal pattern of hunting, preying on particular species in the season in which a combination of the above factors proved the best; and (6) minimize the work involved in returning large-bodied animals to the community.

An example of how we ourselves operate in this fashion may clarify the logic behind the argument. Most of us rely on modern supermarkets to supply our food needs. Supermarkets fulfill items 2 and 3 above by eliminating the "search time" required to locate food and by concentrating most of the food at one location, thereby cutting down on the distance traveled. We generally buy locally processed foods as opposed to imported goods because of the lower cost of the former, which corresponds to item 1 above. Likewise, we choose items, particularly in selecting produce goods, that are in season, as these foods are either inferior in quality or exorbitantly priced at other times of the year.

Given these expectations, we would anticipate the following patterns to be present archaeologically; (a) greater dependence on larger-bodied animals; (b) species to be taken in proportion to their potential frequency of occurrence in the canyon—it takes less time to locate more abundant species; (c) greater emphasis on the one species among similar sized species that occurs closest to the community; (d) greater dependence on species that herd or live in communities, as opposed to solitary or nocturnal species; (e) the ages of the animals present to reflect the ages of the animal community during their seasonal periods of abundance for small animals and of aggregation for large animals, or during their "fattest" seasons; and (f) the pattern of large mammal body parts present in the communities to reflect those sections yielding the most meat, and potential for use as tools, or for marrow or bone grease. Marrow, found in the interior of bone shafts, and bone grease, recovered from the bone tissue itself, were possibly important sources of fat and other nutrients.

During periods of resource scarcities, these patterns could break down for any one of several reasons; the gradual depletion of large game animals, pressure from more critical agricultural activities, or the pressure of human population growth on the available resources of the canyon. As a result we would expect that the optimal strategy we have outlined might not have been followed.

The next two sections of this paper explore the degree to which the data from the sites fit our expectations. The section on hunting strategies deals with evaluating the first five expectations. The section on methods of animal processing concerns the sixth expectation and other facets of the cultural behavior of the groups discernable from the faunal remains.

HUNTING STRATEGIES

Examination of any group's hunting behavior requires an understanding of what species are potentially available, their relative abundance, and the behavior of these species. In an inland area, hunting would center on mammals and birds. The variety of available mammalian fauna can be seen by examining Table 5, which lists those species present in the Sandias today and in the recent past. The diversity in avian fauna is also great (see species list), though a comprehensive list of species of the Sandias is unavailable (see Ligon 1961 for lists of species present in central New Mexico).

The remains of mammals encountered at the three sites examined in this paper are also listed in Table 5. Of the 73 species found in or near the Sandias, only 40 are present in at least one of the sites, with only 12, 19, and 21 species represented by more than one or a few bones at Coconito, Tijeras Pueblo, and San Antonio, respectively. A wide variety of species were exploited by the people at each site, but a selective process of some sort was carried out and is understandable in light of our expectations. The nonexploited species and those represented by few bones are, not

TABLE 5. Comparison of Mammalian Species Occurring in the Sandia Mountains to Those Recovered at the Coconito, Tijeras Pueblo, and San Antonio Sites*

Common or General Name	Species	Sandia Mts.	Coconito	Tijeras Pueblo	San Antonio
shrews	Sorex vagrans	X			
	Sorex nanus	X			
	Sorex merriami	X			
bats	Myotis thysanodes	X			
	Myotis auriculus	X			
	Myotis volans	X			
	Lasiurus cinereus	X			
	Epesticus fuscus	X			
	Lasiurus cinereus	X			
	Plecotus townsendii	X			
	Antrozous pallidus	X			
	Tadarida brasiliensis	X			
eastern cottontail	Sylvilagus floridanus			X	X
desert cottontail	Sylvilagus auduboni	X	?	X	X
Rocky Mountain cottontail	Sylvilagus nuttalli	X	?	X	X
jack rabbit	Lepus californicus	X	X	X	X
chipmunks	Eutamias minimus	X		X+	X
	Eutamias quarrivitatus	X			
ground squirrels	Ammospermophilus interpres	X			
	Spermophilus pilosma	X	X	X	X
	Spermophilus variegatus	X		X	X
prairie dogs	Cynomys gunnisoni	X		X	X
	Cynomys ludovicianus	X		X	X
tree squirrels	Sciurus aberti	X			X
	Sciurus niger•a		X		X
	Tamiascirus hudsonicus	X			
pocket gophers	Thomomys bottae	X	X	X	X
	Geomys•			X+	
pocket mice	Perognathus flavus	X			
	Perognathus hispidus	X			
	Perognathus intermedius	X			

mice	Reithrodom tomysmontanus	X			
	Reithrodontomys megalotis	X			
	Peromyscus maniculatus	X			
	Peromyscus leucopus	X			
	Peromyscus boylii	X			
	Peromyscus truei	X			
	Peromyscus difficilis	X			
	Peromyscus sp.[b]	X	X	X	X
	Onychomys leucogaster	X			X
rats	Sigmodon hispidus[*]				
	Sigmodon fluviventer[*]		X		X
	Neotoma micropus	X			
	Neotoma albigula	X	X	X	X
	Neotoma mexicana	X		X+	
voles	Microtus longicaudus	X		X+	
	Microtus sp.[b]	X		X	
muskrat	Ondatra zebethicus	X	X	X	X
porcupine	Erethizon dorsatum	X		X	X
coyote	Canis latrans	X	X	X	X
Gray wolf	Canis lupus				X
fox	Vulpes sp.[b]	X			X
gray fox	Urocyon cinereoargenteus	X		X+	X
black bear	Ursus americanus	X	X	X	X
ringtail	Basseriscus astutus	X			
raccoon	Procyn lotor	X			
badger	Tacidea taxus	X	X	X	X
skunks	Spilogale gracilis	X			
	Metphitis peohitis	X		X+	X
	Cenopattus mesoleucus	X			
mountain lion	Felis concolor[*]	X		X	X
bobcat	Lynx rufus	X		X	X
elk (wapiti)	Cervus elephus[*]			X	X
mule deer	Odcoileus hemionus	X	X	X	X
pronghorn antelope	Antilocapra americana	X	X	X	X
Rocky Mountain bighorn	Ovis canadensis	X		X	X
bison	Bison bison		X		X

*These items and the San Antonio and Coconito columns are not from Cordell (1977:455).

+ These species identified from areas not yet examined at the time of Cordell's research (1977).

a. This species does not occur in the canyon. The remains may have been misidentified and could belong instead to Abert's Squirrel.

b. These general categories represent remains that could not be speciated.

surprisingly, animals such as bats, shrews, some small rodents, and carnivores. The exploitation of these small, nocturnal, or solitary animals would involve labor costs exceeding their return in meat. This observation partially supports the first, second, and third expectations.

A complete list of bird species recovered from the sites is unavailable as the researchers were unable adequately to speciate bird remains other than turkey, but we have a partial list of those species identified. As a class avian fauna are much less abundant in the remains than are the mammals. This is to be expected considering the difficulty in capturing birds, their migratory behavior, and their limited seasonal availability. Turkey, the one species consistently found at all three sites, is an exception because

Partial List of the Bird Species Present at Tijeras Pueblo

*cf. *Anas diazi* (New Mexican duck)
 cf. *Anas platyrhynchos* (mallard)
    Spatula clypeata (shovellor)
 cf. *Buteo swainsoni* (Swainson's hawk)
    Buteo regalis (ferruginous hawk)
 cf. *Accipiter cooperii* (Copper's hawk)
 cf. *Circus cyaneus* (March hawk)
 cf. *Lophortyx gambeli* (Gamble quail)
    Callipepla squamata (Arizona scaled quail)
    Grus canadensis (sand hill crane)
 cf. *Zenaidura macroura* (western mourning dove)
    Speotyto cunicularia (burrowing owl)
    Asio otus (long-eared owl)
 cf. *Cassidix mexicanus* (great-tailed grackle)
    Colaptus cafer (red-shafted flicker)
    Sphyrapicus varius (yellow-bellied sapsucker)
 cf. *Nucifraga columbiana* (Clark's nutcracker)
 cf. *Cyanocitta stelleri* (long-crested jay)
 cf. *Gynmorhinus cyanocephalus* (piñyon jay)
 cf. *Tyrannus tyrannus* (eastern kingbird)
    Turdus migratorius (robin)
 cf. *Meleagris gallapavo* (turkey)

 cf. = approximately the size of

of its larger size, year-round availability, and particularly, its partially ground-dwelling behavior and the possibility that it was partially domesticated. Many of the other bird species identified also exhibit one or more of these characteristics.

Preliminary observations then, tell us something about what species were hunted and why, but little about what species were depended on consistently for food. To infer the latter, we must examine the relative proportions of the species at each site. Tables 6–8 list these proportions, as well as the total number of bones found per species and the Minimum Number of Individuals for each occupation at the three sites. Minimum Number of Individuals (MNI) is defined as the smallest number of animals necessary to account for the number of bones found.

To understand what the proportions might mean in terms of hunting strategies, it is necessary to look more closely at the relative abundance of the species in the canyon. Knowledge of the life zones they occupy will help in understanding the distance traveled to exploit that game. Knowledge of a species' distribution in the area, and of their behavior patterns, helps in determining the likelihood of capture on any one outing, and the method of capture most likely to be used. Such information is necessary to assess, however crudely, the relative degree of energy spent in hunting between different groups and periods. Limitations on space prohibit outlining this information for each species. (See Young 1978 for summaries of this information per species, derived primarily from Findley et al. 1975, and, secondarily, from Bailey 1932 and Cordell 1977.)

Though their relative frequency varies slightly between sites and occupations, cottontails consistently rank first in relation to all other animals exploited. A possible exception to this is the Early San Antonio period remains. Excavated from a very small area of the site, these remains contained a high concentration of nearly whole turkey skeletons. While this may indicate turkey burials, a phenomenon often encountered in the Southwest, such a high concentration may be biasing the relative frequencies and, in turn, the representation of what was actually consumed on a regular basis.

Although cottontails are relatively small animals, they are abundant throughout the Sandias. Nearly 87 percent of the total acreage of the region is suitable habitat for these rabbits, a potential abundance matched by no other species. The widespread oc-

TABLE 6. Coconito Faunal Remains

Species	Number of bones identified	Minimum number of individuals	Relative freq. (%)
Sylvilagus audoboni	347	20.5	31.8
Lepus californicus	141	7.0	10.8
Spermophilus spilosoma	17	1.5	2.3
Cynomys gunnisoni	52	6.0	9.3
Sciurus niger	3	1.0	1.5
Thomomys bottae	68	13.0	20.2
Dipodomys ordii	1	0.5	0.8
Peromyscus sp.	15	1.0	1.5
Sigmodon fluviventer	3	1.0	1.5
Neotoma albigula	30	2.0	3.1
Onadatra zibethicus	1	0.5	0.8
Canis latrans	2	0.5	0.8
Urocyon cinereoargenteus	7	0.5	0.8
Taxidae taxus	1	0.5	0.8
Odocoileus sp.	111	4.0	6.2
Antilocapra americana	26	1.5	2.3
Bison bison	3	0.5	0.8
Bos taurus[a]	8	1.0	— — —
Meleagris gallapavo	283	3.0	4.6
Crotelus sp.[b]	141	?	— — —

Unidentifiable fragments:	small mammal	1,395
	medium mammal	1,603
	large mammal	257
	small bird	57
	large bird	21

a. All bones of domestic cow were found on or near the surface and outside of archaeological structures, and are considered intrusive.
b. Vertebral bones of rattlesnakes were found in 3 rooms. They were noted as probable burrow deaths
in the Coconito site report (Teglia 1977) and are considered intrusive.

TABLE 7. Tijeras Pueblo Faunal Remains

	EARLY			LATE		
Species	Number of bones identified	MNI	Relative freq. (%)	Number of bones identified	MNI	Relative freq. (%)
Sylvilagus sp. S. audoboni S. floridanus S. nuttalli	969	42.5	31.1	452	26.0	30.9
Lepus californicus cf. Eutamias	264	8.0	5.9	124	5.0	5.9
quadrivittatus	— — —	— — —	— — —	1	0.5	0.6
Spermophilus spilosoma	1	0.5	0.4	2	0.5	0.6
Spermophilus variegatus	36	5.5	4.0	9	1.5	1.8

TABLE 7. Tijeras Pueblo Faunal Remains

	EARLY			LATE		
Species	Number of bones identified	MNI	Relative freq. (%)	Number of bones identified	MNI	Relative freq. (%)
Cynomys sp.	118	9.0	6.6	57	6.0	7.1
C. ludovicianus	73	6.5		21	4.0	
C. gunnisoni	33	2.5		19	1.5	
Sciurus aberti	10	2.0	1.5	———	———	———
Thomomys bottae	84	21.0	15.4	76	19.5	23.2
Geomys sp.	24	5.5	4.0	2	1.0	1.2
cf. *Reithrodontomys* sp.	2	1.0	0.7	———	———	———
Peromyscus sp./ *Onychomy leucogaster*	43	7.5	5.5	6	1.0	1.2
P. sp.	32	7.0		2	0.5	
O. leucogaster	1	0.5		———	———	———
Neotoma sp.	47	7.0	5.1	43	4.5	5.4
Microtus sp.	1	0.5	0.4	2	0.5	0.6
Erethizon dorsatum	18	1.0	0.7	3	0.5	0.6
Canis latrans/familiaris	2	0.5	0.4	6	0.5	0.6
Vulpes sp.	4	1.0	0.7	4	0.5	0.6
Urocyon cinereoargenteus	25	1.0	0.7	16	1.0	1.2
Ursus americanus	1	0.5	0.4	1	0.5	0.6
Mustela frenata	1	0.5	0.4	———	———	———
Taxidae taxus	3	0.5	0.4	5	0.5	0.6
Mephitis mephitis	———	———	———	2	0.5	0.6
Lynx rufus	10	0.5	0.4	11	1.0	1.2
Cervus elaphus	9	0.5	0.4	———	———	———
Odocoileus sp.	223	5.0	3.7	173	3.0	3.6
Antilocapra americana	273	6.0	4.4	104	2.5	3.0
Bison bison	16	0.5	0.4	———	———	———
Ovis canadensis	9	1.0	0.7	14	0.5	0.6
Meleagris gallopavo	546	8.0	5.9	130	6.5	7.7
Crotelus sp.	———	———	———	14	0.5	———

Number of bones identified to a higher taxonomic level

EARLY

Sciuridae = 33
Geomydae = 4
Felid Lynx = 4
Small mammal = 41
Medium mammal = 44
Small artiodactyl = 363
Large Artiodactyl = 20
Small bird = 46
Medium bird = 64
Large bird = 10

Unidentifiable fragments = not quantified

LATE

Sciuridae = 29
Felid Lynx rufus = 2
Small mammal = 14
Medium mammal = 17
Small Artiodactyl = 123
Large Artiodactyl = 4
Small bird = [+]12
Medium bird = [+]5

Unidentifiable fragments = not quantified

TABLE 8. San Antonio Faunal Remains

	EARLY			MIDDLE			LATE-MIDDLE			17th CENTURY		
	Number of bones identified	MNI	Relative freq. (%)	Number of bones identified	MNI	Relative freq. (%)	Number of bones identified	MNI	Relative freq. (%)	Number of bones identified	MNI	Relative freq. (%)
Sylvilagus sp.	60	3.0	14.0	346	12.5	22.9	133	6.5	30.9	111	4.0	19.0
S. audoboni	2	0.5	—	14	1.0	—	9	1.0	—	3	0.5	—
S. floridanus	9	1.0	4.7	98	2.5	4.6	25	1.0	4.9	27	1.0	4.8
Lepus californicus	1	0.5	2.3	14	4.5	8.3	2	0.5	2.4	1	0.5	2.4
Spermophilus spilosoma	—	—	—	4	1.0	1.8	—	—	—	1	0.5	2.4
Spermophilus variegatus	9	1.5	7.0	37	4.5	8.3	8	1.0	4.9	15	3.0	14.3
Cynomys sp.	—	—	—	5	0.5	0.9	—	—	—	2	0.5	2.4
C. ludovicianus	9	1.5	—	32	4.5	—	8	1.0	—	13	2.5	—
C. gunnisoni	2	0.5	2.3	5	1.5	2.7	1	0.5	2.4	—	—	—
Sciurus niger/aberti	3	1.5	7.0	18	6.0	11.0	8	1.0	4.9	4	1.0	4.8
Thomomys bottae	—	—	—	1	0.5	0.9	—	—	—	—	—	—
Geomys sp.	—	—	—	1	0.5	0.9	—	—	—	—	—	—
cf. Dip ordii	—	—	—	25	3.0	5.5	1	0.5	2.4	1	0.5	2.4
Peromyscus sp.	11	1.5	7.0	3	1.0	1.8	13	2.5	12.2	—	—	—
Sigmodon hispidus	5	1.0	4.7	9	1.5	2.7	—	—	—	1	0.5	2.4
Neotoma albigula	—	—	—	—	—	—	4	0.5	2.4	5	1.0	4.8
Microtus sp.[a]	19	0.5	2.3	1	0.5	0.9	—	—	—	—	—	—
Ondatra zibethicus	—	—	—	5	1.0	1.8	—	—	—	—	—	—
Erethizon dorsatum	3	1.0	4.7	2	0.5	0.9	1	0.5	2.4	—	—	—
Canis latrans/familiaris	—	—	—	1	0.5	0.9	—	—	—	—	—	—
Felis concolor	—	—	—	1	0.5	0.9	—	—	—	—	—	—
Felis domesticus[b]	—	—	—	—	—	—	—	—	—	1	0.5	2.4
Lynx rufus	1	0.5	2.3	3	0.5	0.9	—	—	—	—	—	—
Odocoileus sp.	2	0.5	2.3	35	1.5	2.7	25	1.0	4.9	22	1.5	7.1

Taxon												
Antilocapra americana	6	0.5	2.3	37	3.0	5.5	42	3.0	14.6	43	2.0	4.8
Bison bison	—	—	—	—	—	—	1	0.5	2.4	1	0.5	2.4
Ovis canadensis	—	—	—	1	0.5	0.9	—	—	—	—	—	—
Bos taurus[b]	—	—	—	1	0.5	—	—	—	—	—	—	—
Ovis aries/Capra hirca[b]	—	—	—	1	0.5	—	—	—	—	—	—	—
Meleagris gallupavo	283	6.0	28.0	179	7.0	12.8	51	1.5	7.3	46	2.0	9.5
Crotelus sp.	37	?	—	194	?	—	—	—	—	—	—	—
Catostomidae	—	—	—	2	0.5	0.9	—	—	—	—	—	—

small artiodactyl[b] = 7
large artiodactyl = 1

unidentifiable fragments = 432

cf. *Lepus/Sylvilagus* = 14
small-medium rodent = 3
cf. small carnivore = 15
small artiodactyl[b] = 156
large artiodactyl = 7

unidentifiable fragments = 765

small-medium rodent = 3
cf. small carnivore = 1
small artiodactyl[b] = 95
large artiodactyl = 7

unidentifiable fragments = 334

cf. *Lepus/Sylvilagus* = 8
small-medium rodent = 3
cf. small carnivore = 4
small artiodactyl[b] = 76
large artiodactyl = 8

unidentifiable fragments = 343

a. Mouse remains are considered intrusive and are not included in the relative frequencies.
b. The dometic cow, sheep, and goat remains are believed to be intrusive and are not included in the relative frequencies.

currence of cottontails would correspond to our expectations of minimizing search time, cutting down on distance traveled to hunt, and insuring the capture of something on any one outing. The seasonal peaks in cottontail population size (early spring and late summer) may have corresponded to agricultural lean periods when stored winter supplies were low and the harvest not in. Although we cannot show that these were the seasons when rabbits were hunted, cottontails could easily have filled food deficit periods while minimally interfering with agricultural activities.

At first glance, the consistently lower frequency of jackrabbits— a genus of rabbit twice the size of cottontails—appears to conflict with our expectations. It is understandable that this species ranks fifth in importance though, when its habitat is examined. Jackrabbits favor the foothill grasslands and mesas adjacent to the mountains, a potential habitat of only 12 percent in the Sandias. Thus, the distance traveled to exploit jackrabbits negates the advantage of their greater body size relative to cottontails. The higher frequency of jackrabbits at Coconito may be due to the canyon-bottom location of the site and its proximity to this rabbit's habitat. Data on the practices of late nineteenth century and early twentieth century puebloan groups (Linsky 1974) suggest that jackrabbits, unlike cottontails, were more effectively taken by larger groups of hunters than by single individuals. Cooperative hunts, then, would entail a greater energy cost than the return in meat would merit.

The frequencies of pocket gophers and the larger-bodied prairie dogs cannot be examined as easily as that of the rabbits. These burrowing animals, particularly pocket gophers, inhabit areas that depend more on the friability of various soils than on types of vegetation cover. Prairie dogs may have been less abundant in the immediate area of the sites than pocket gophers, because their habitats are more restricted by particular topographic features. The greater frequency of pocket gophers in the Tijeras Pueblo and the Coconito occupations may be a result of elevational differences. These animals occur in greater numbers in the Upper Sonoran life zone, the zone where these sites are located. Some pocket gophers may be the remains of intrusive animals; animals that became residents of the site after human abandonment. The consistent recovery of only mandibles for this species, however, seems to indicate that no more than a few are intrusive. The relative proportion of these rodents, then, may be slightly inflated in some or all of the occupation levels.

The other rodents recovered generally occur sporadically or in low frequency. There are several ways we can explain the presence of these rodents at the sites; they may have been captured as "byproducts" of rabbit hunts (Beaglehole 1936), trapped around the sites as an expedient food source, or as pests, attracted to the site by inefficient food storage containers. In any event, their small size and the sporadic occurrence would imply that no particular species was systematically exploited for meat. The high proportion of rock squirrels relative to spotted ground squirrels only at Tijeras Pueblo may, again, be the result of the site's proximity to the animal's habitat. Rock squirrels favor rocky outcrops which partially surround Tijeras Pueblo.

The combined proportion of these smaller rodents ranges from 7 percent to nearly 24 percent of the minimum number of individuals. The greatest proportions occur in the Early Tijeras, San Antonio Middle, and San Antonio Late Middle periods (17.6 percent, 21.5 percent, and 23.7 percent, respectively). The possible significance of high proportions in these periods will be discussed in the summary of this section. Again, any or all of these rodents may be intrusive, but at present we have no sure way of testing this. Cut marks on a small number of rodent bones have been recorded at San Antonio and Tijeras Pueblo, indicating that at least some of the rodents were used as food, but the exact proportion is unknown.

The relationships among the various species of artiodactyls— deer, antelope, bighorn sheep, bison, and elk—represent the greatest variation from our expectations. Based on the proportion of potential habitat area available in the region for each of these species, deer should far outnumber any other species. The sporadic occurrence of bighorn sheep and bison is expected, as both have restricted ranges on the fringes or outside of the Sandias proper.

The single occurrence of elk remains, at Tijeras Pueblo, is not surprising. The habitat of elk, high montane grasslands, does not occur in the Sandias, so it is doubtful that this species was present in the area. It is possible, however, that elk were taken during infrequent hunts in the nearby Jemez or Sangre de Cristo mountains, areas within their present and previous range.

Coconito and the seventeenth-century occupation of San Antonio are the only instances where the remains of deer and antelope even faintly correspond to the expected relationship. Antelope outnumber deer in the three roughly contemporary occupations between sites—the Middle and Late Middle periods of San Antonio and the Early occupation of Tijeras Pueblo. It is difficult to understand why antelope—which are only half the size of deer, occur mainly on the outskirts of the canyon, and, unlike deer, generally require communal hunting efforts—occur in greater relative proportions than deer.

Cordell (1977:459) has provided two possible explanations for this phenomenon. The human population density in the canyon was probably higher at this time than at any point before. The relative abundance of deer may have been inadvertently reduced by extensive land clearing of their habitat for agricultural purposes. The reduction of habitat seems an unlikely explanation if we look at the frequency of cottontail, a species whose range partially coincides with deer. Cottontails should decrease in importance relative to jackrabbits during these periods, if the former's habitat was destroyed, but they do not.

The second explanation also cites the high population density of the canyon as a factor in the unexpectedly high exploitation of antelope. The greater number of people inhabiting the canyon made larger hunting groups feasible. Intervillage cooperative hunting groups could more easily exploit antelope herds of the Estancia Basin, the western bajada of the Sandias, or the meadowlands near Paa-ko. Since antelope inhabit such open areas, a large group of hunters must surround an entire herd, conducting a form of drive, to successfully capture them. One advantage of this method would be the greater number of animals taken in one outing.

Deer, which occur in small groups primarily in the wooded areas of the Sandias, can most often only be taken singly, but many fewer individual hunters or small hunting teams are required to take a deer than to capture an antelope. It is not possible to compare the cost of a given quantity of meat returned by the individual deer hunter with that returned by the communal antelope drive. But when all factors involved in hunting are considered, the communal effort may have required the greater energy demands. It is possible, though, that several benefits of intervillage or communal hunting may have offset this seeming disadvantage, making the practice more "cost effective" in the long run. The nature of these possible advantages is discussed in the summary of this section.

Determining the time of year artiodactyls were hunted is nearly impossible for the remains of community sites in general. Some evidence, however, partially refutes our expectation of fall hunting. In each of the occupations, bones of foetal deer and antelope were recovered. The presence of foetal animals implies that some hunting occurred in the late winter or early spring, the time of year when females are pregnant. The relatively high proportions of foetal individuals in some periods suggest that spring hunting may have been substantial. All we can say with certainty is that hunting of these large mammals was not restricted to fall, the season assumed to be optimal.

The carnivores consistently are the least exploited animals in all periods, equal in numbers only to a few smaller rodents and, occasionally, the rare bison, bighorn, and elk. As mentioned earlier, the lower proportion of carnivores is due to their solitary and evasive behavior. Also, carnivores should be less abundant than even the larger herbivores because of their higher position in the food chain. Both Tijeras occupations show a greater variety of carnivores, which may be a result of the larger sample size analyzed from this site than from the others.

The reasons for the likelihood of hunting turkey have already been mentioned, but variations in the degree of exploitation between sites are worth noting. The slight differences in proportion of this seemingly favored species may be related to the respective elevations of each site. The lower limit of the turkey's range is 6,000 feet, just below the elevation of San Antonio, the site highest in elevation of the three examined. It is at San Antonio that the greatest proportion of turkeys was taken, even considering the questionable porportions discussed earlier for the Early period. Tijeras Pueblo and Coconito, both lower in elevation, have lower proportions of turkey. Distance traveled to obtain turkey may be the relevant variable influencing the degree of dependence evident at each site.

Alternatively, the turkeys at these sites may have been domesticated. Although wild turkeys were abundant in the past, they are difficult to capture once preyed upon, as they quickly become

wary of predators. These birds were domesticated very early in the
prehistory of the Southwest, so it is not unreasonable to assume
they were kept at the sites in Tijeras Canyon. Distinguishing wild
from prehistoric domestic turkeys anatomically is very difficult
and was not attempted. We have no evidence of pen structures
that could have been used for turkeys. The presence of possible
turkey burials at all three sites, however, may be some clue that
these animals were kept, as a food source, for feathers, and for
other purposes. If they were domesticated, elevational differences
would have no effect on the variations in turkey proportions present. Domestication would, to some degree, insure that a certain
supply of meat is readily available. Perhaps the need for this insur-
ance was greater at San Antonio than at Tijeras or Coconito.

Summary: The species hunted during each period seem to
reflect either the relative abundance of the species in the canyon,
its proximity to a particular site, or the ease of its capture. These
patterns agree with the first four expectations. The reversal of the
expected relationship between deer and antelope in the Middle
and Late Middle San Antonio periods and the Early Tijeras period
is the only major deviation. As for our fifth expectation, we lack
adequate methods to evaluate the time of year of hunting. The evidence we do have appears to negate the consistent practices of fall
hunting for the larger, more economically important animals.

A possible explanation for the odd relationship between deer
and antelope suggested that intervillage cooperative hunts
allowed the exploitation of the slightly more distant antelope
herds. This practice may have demanded more time and energy
than hunting deer, but possible residual benefits may have made
the antelope drives worth their effort. Given some of the evidence
we have from these periods (Middle and Late Middle San Antonio,
and Early Tijeras Pueblo), we can begin to infer what these benefits might have been and possibly how effective they were.

We are fairly certain that these occupations were roughly contemporary. We are also fairly sure that a greater number of people
inhabited Tijeras Canyon during this time than at any other prehistoric period. These occupations are also the periods with the
highest combined frequencies of small rodents. Whether the
rodents were taken as expedient food sources or as agricultural
pests, the majority were probably consumed. The greater number

of rodents, then, represents a break from the more efficient hunting strategies of the earlier periods at Coconito and the later seventeenth century at San Antonio. Given the probable instability of agricultural yields in general, and the co-occurrence of the increase in rodent use with the greater number of people in the canyon at this time, we might infer that these groups were finding it difficult to make ends meet.

One way to alleviate a real or anticipated lack of resources is to have some knowledge of where the available wild, scattered resources are at any given time. Maintaining regular intervillage hunts would be a good vehicle for enhancing the exchange of such information between communities within the canyon. Intervillage ceremonials, even modern-day state and county fairs, function in a similar manner by offering opportunities to exchange information. Using a few hunters from each community to form an adequate-sized group to conduct drives, as opposed to sending independent hunting parties from each village, may also have been an advantage to the people. The former reduces the number of individuals absent from each community at a given time and does not disrupt other, equally important activities. When these potential benefits are considered, the greater effort of hunting antelope could have been a necessity to the survival of the two communities.

This discussion is, of course, largely speculation. One of the problems in the argument is the assumption that Tijeras Canyon populations of these periods were in fact deficient in agricultural resources. Two factors, independent of the faunal data, may lend some credibility to our findings. A significant incidence of iron-deficiency anemia occurred in the most vulnerable age/sex groups of Tijeras Pueblo and other communities (see Ferguson, this volume). The most probable cause of this disease seems to be a lack of meat protein. Although we're not certain of the exact period to which the diseased individuals belong, it seems reasonable to assume that one or all of the Tijeras groups were experiencing some difficulty in obtaining adequate supplies of meat.

Second, following the occupations in question, both Tijeras and San Antonio were abandoned. The Tijeras site, after a second, brief occupation by a smaller community, was permanently abandoned, and San Antonio remained unoccupied for a span of four centuries. The faunal remains do not in any way supply the cause for abandonment, as no drastic meat shortages are apparent. The abandonments do indicate that the people's methods of obtaining a livelihood were becoming less viable in some way.

The faunal data do not indicate any drastic changes in hunting behavior during the entire span of prehistoric occupation. Suggestions of an increased input of energy for the amount of food obtained toward the end of the canyon's prehistory have been noted. If the assumptions are correct, this implies a breakdown of the expected, more efficient hunting strategy. A less efficient hunting strategy may reflect inadequate agricultural yields for the number of people present in the canyon, necessitating increased demands for hunting and gathering. The aggregation of people into two large communities may not have been a viable strategy to meet the population's food needs, even with the implied benefits of the organization of antelope drives. Reorganization of some of the people into smaller communities, such as the later group at Tijeras, may also have proved inadequate. Scarce food resources may have led to the abandonment of sites and, for centuries, the entire canyon.

METHODS OF ANIMAL PROCESSING

Investigation of the hunting strategies of various groups is only one facet of studying prehistoric subsistence methods from animal remains. Determining the butchering patterns of specific animals, delimiting evidence for the storage or immediate use of meat, and inferring the particular by-product uses of the bones can lead to a better understanding of the importance of animal products to the communities studied. (See Young 1978 for a description of the methods used in examining the faunal remains in this section.)

Again we need first to outline what we would expect the pattern of remains to look like in order to impart some sort of meaning to what is actually found. In terms of conserving human energy, we would expect large-bodied animals to be partially butchered at or near the area where they were killed. This eliminates transporting the unnecessary weight of nonusable body parts to the community sites. The body parts found at the site, then, should be those parts considered valuable for their high meat return, high marrow content, and suitability for use in making tools. The upper leg and the rump and breast areas are highest in meat value; the upper limb bones have a high marrow content; and the metapodials are a good source of tool material (Figure 43).

The value of particular body parts would change depending on the group's assessment of its needs. For instance, in periods of resource abundance, only the choicest parts might be utilized. When food is less abundant, we would expect greater use of each animal and that portions of the meat would be dried for storage.

Smaller animals, such as rabbits, rodents, and turkeys, should be relatively whole at the site. The difference between their live and dressed weights is not great enough to make any initial processing an advantage. As only the meat of these smaller animals is

43. Bone artifacts, including a flute (center), recovered from Tijeras Pueblo.

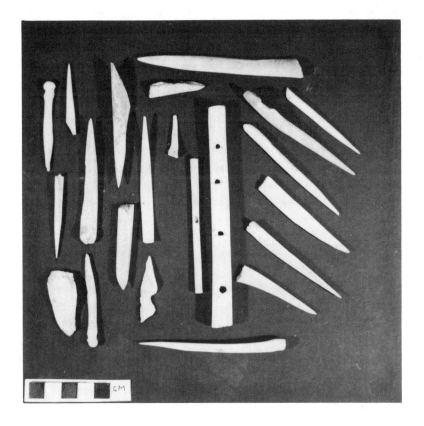

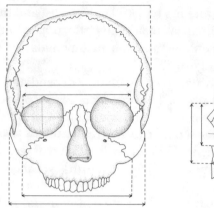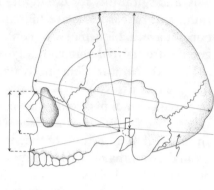

44. Traditional measurements of skull dimensions.

nutritionally important, we would not expect to find indications of bone cracked for marrow as is typical with deer and antelope. Use of the slender long bones of turkey and rabbits for delicate working tools and as ornaments would be the factor most likely to cause incompleteness of these remains at the sites (Figure 43).

Discerning the patterns of use of animal remains is not as easy as one might think. Any single bone may have undergone a partial or total metamorphosis from the point when it was removed from the freshly killed animal to its final disposal by a human user. Each successive treatment of the bone could have masked or obliterated scars of its previous use or leave it with no recognizable mark at all. We know that not all types of bones were processed in the same manner, nor was any one element subjected to all types of uses. We suspect that each bone was processed according to its particular characteristic—its physical structure, its contents, and its surrounding meat.

Alteration of bones does not end when they are discarded. Chemical and physical weathering processes may affect or destroy the bone while it is on the surface or buried in the soil. Weathering processes are not random, but depend on the density and completeness of the bone at the time of its disposal. As the climate and soils of much of the Southwest offer excellent preservation conditions, it is fairly certain that natural decay is not the major factor affecting the types of body parts recovered. To test this assumption, the pattern of artiodactyl remains recovered from various periods was compared to the patterns that might be expected if the bones had suffered normal decay (Binford and Bertram 1977). Significant difference occurred between the two sets of data, assuring that natural causes were not the sole determinants of the observed pattern of body parts recovered.

In order to assess the degree to which the large mammals were processed before returning them to the community sites, the body parts consistently absent from the sites or found in low frequency were noted. In all periods, all portions of the vertebral column are very low in number or totally absent. Vertebral ends of ribs are equally scarce, though the shafts of ribs are quite numerous. In every case, nearly all the vertebral fragments present are of immature individuals, as are most of the few skull fragments found. Besides these, no other complex of bones is entirely absent, consistently low in frequency, or totally comprised of immature individuals. The degree of initial processing, then, was probably minimal, involving the removal of only the spinal column by breaking the ribs below their attachments to the vertebrae, separating the lower column from the pelvis at the sacrum, and dividing the animal into manageable "packages" for transport. Immature animals were probably returned to the site whole. Young animals would, of course, be lighter than adults and easier to carry over an equal distance. Very little of the adult animal's potential products were left to waste at the processing site, since even the body parts of lesser value were apparently also returned to the site for use.

Preparation Methods

If meat was to be processed for storage, it could have been prepared either at the kill site or at the community site. In a semi-arid climate, the process would involve stripping the meat from the unbroken bone and removing the moisture by hanging it in a tree or on a rack. The meat is dried by either the sun or a smoke fire, much in the way jerky is prepared, though without the aid of special ovens. Once dried, the meat will store for several months. Drying leaves no mark on the bone, making it impossible to distinguish between storage or immediate consumption of meat.

If the meat were so processed at the kill site, one might expect the stripped bones to be absent or underrepresented at the pueblo sites. As mentioned earlier, no bones are absent nor consistently low in frequency with the exception of the vertebral column. This does not imply, however, that meat was not stored. The bones may have been returned to the site whole and later cracked for marrow, or the meat may have been dried at the community sites.

There is one bit of evidence against the regular storage of meat during any period. The breast meat surrounding the ribs is the optimal meat for storage. Once a rib, or any bone, is broken, the meat around it spoils within a short time. If the head ends of ribs were, in fact, left attached to the vertebral column at the kill site, the ribs would certainly have been broken immediately, leading to the rapid putrification of the meat. The broken ribs, then, indicate that meat was generally consumed soon after the animal was killed.

The reasons meat storage may not have been practiced are obscure. Food storage is an artificial means of increasing the length of time a resource is available and so would have greatly enhanced the group's food security. The optimal times to store food would be when the animals are fattest and prior to a period when it would be most needed—both being early to late fall. This is also the season when the bulk of corn harvesting is done and piñon gathering is under way. Both of these activities require large labor forces and may involve more physical work than hunting. Corn and piñon require virtually no processing for storage and are reliable. A risk of failure is inherent in trying to procure enough animals to make processing meat worth the effort. In the event of such a scheduling conflict, the plant foods were probably chosen. As a last resort, meat may have been stored in years of poor agricultural yields, but there are no archaeological methods to discern the occurrence of poor years.

Once returned to the site, fresh meat could have been prepared for consumption by either boiling or roasting. Roasting is the only method that would leave some archaeologically discernable mark, such as charring of the bone edge or of the interior of a broken bone. Char marks were absent on the remains of all periods.

An inferential method of determining whether boiling was the regular cooking method was attempted, and proved successful. We assumed that if the meat attached to bone were usually boiled, the size of bones lacking high marrow content should be fairly uniform, reflecting the size of the cooking vessel. A consistent size would not be necessary if the meat had been roasted, as the segments of the animal cooked could be skewered and not have to conform to any particular size or shape. In order to test this notion, the lengths of rib shaft fragments were recorded from each period of the three sites. The average size is strikingly similar for all occupations, ranging from 6.10 to 7.11 cm. Although measurements were not taken on other non-marrow-bearing bones, the pelvis and scapula fragments recovered were consistently broken in a manner yielding similarly sized fragments. Such patterning indicates the practice of reducing meat with bone to fit into cooking vessels. It seems likely, then, that the meat of the larger animals was generally boiled.

Although an expectation of the probable cooking method had not been established, the boiling of meat fits well with what is already known about these community groups. Boiling allows food to cook for long periods without constant attention. It is thought to be an efficient technique for preparing foods among sedentary peoples as it permits members of the group both to cook and to be available to engage in other tasks during peak activity periods of the day (Glassow 1972:287). Boiling meat on the bones would also be a way to retrieve all the available nutrients from animal products. Employing such a cooking method may well have been a necessity for groups constrained for both time and resources, a situation suggested by the rest of the analysis.

To determine if marrow or bone grease was extracted from any or all of the large mammal bones at these sites, an outline of the processing stages is needed. Accounts of contemporary groups recorded by anthropologists in the field describe the following method (Vehik 1978; Yellen 1977). The particular bones selected for marrow cracking are those highest in marrow content, such as the upper limb bones. The use of other long bones varies, depending largely on the size of the species. For example, marrow may be taken from the lower leg bones of a buffalo, while marrow from the same part of an antelope will not. The elements selected for making bone grease from animals the size of deer and antelope are not mentioned, though it is implied that all long bones are suitable. Marrow and bone grease contain important nutrients and are high in calories. It is very likely, though not mentioned in the accounts, that the types of bones used might vary with the needs of the groups.

After the meat is removed, the selected bones may or may not be heated to remove the outer filmlike sheath surrounding each bone. The bone shafts are then cracked in a regular fashion (the exact method of cracking and the resulting fragment size varies) to expose the interior, nearly liquid marrow. The marrow is removed and either eaten immediately or put in a container and set aside. The ends of the bones (epiphyses) can be chopped into small pieces to remove the marrow isolated in them, or left intact if the amount of marrow in them is considered negligible. If the bone is to be further used to make bone grease, the shaft and sometimes the bone ends are smashed into very small fragments, as are selected whole bones not cracked for marrow. These fragments are placed in a pot of boiling water, sometimes with stewing meat, to release the fatty grease from within the bone tissue. The ends of bones left intact from the initial marrow processing may also be thrown into the pot. The marrow which had been set aside can be added to the grease broth to thicken it.

Evaluation of Remains

From these processing steps, one may assume the archaeological remains of bones cracked for marrow would always be fragmentary or reduced to unidentifiable fragments. All bone remnants from processing would presumably wind up in the trash middens or be discarded in rooms or around outdoor eating areas. Conceivably they could be recovered through field excavation.

Of the deer and antelope remains in our samples, no complete long bones were found except a few foetal individuals which would not have been processed. In all periods, the least frequently occurring long bone ends are generally those portions highest in marrow content; the proximal humerus, one or both ends of the femur, and the proximal tibia. The relative frequencies of these bones and of the other long bone ends are generally low, but do vary to some degree between periods and between species within a single period. This variation is probably a result of sampling problems rather than extensive processing.

Although the fragments of long bone found were not measured, the bone ends generally are simply that—epiphyses with little or no shaft attached. Identifiable shaft fragments, those large enough to establish the anatomical position, are very rare. Consistent spiral fracture patterns, evidence of marrow cracking, were noted on these shaft fragments, on some of the long bone ends, and on the elements lower in marrow content. Jagged, splintered edges, probable evidence of smashing, were also noted on all types of long bones. Unfortunately, the extent of these patterns on the remains is unknown, as breakage patterns were not recorded by all researchers.

Based on what has been presented, a greater variety of bone types were probably processed to retrieve marrow and bone grease than expected. The use of bones other than the optimal types may indicate the need of the groups to retrieve all available nutrients possible from the resources at hand.

The proportions of body parts present among the rabbits and turkeys show that these animals were not nearly as anatomically complete as expected. Body representation within species between sites and periods was consistent, but when species are compared the pattern differs somewhat. This patterning is also true for the smaller rodents and the factor or factors influencing it are unknown. Differential recovery of bones may in part affect the pattern, but is is unlikely to be the sole cause. The missing bones were often the larger ones. As expected, the patterns do not fit those for the artiodactyls. The amount of marrow or bone grease available from rabbits and turkeys is miniscule, and so would not be expected to influence the types of bones recovered.

An examination of bone artifacts from each site may give some clues as to how the missing types of bones may have been used. From a small sample of the worked bone recovered from San Antonio and Tijeras, we know that certain turkey and small mammal long bones were shaped into awls and beads, though this use would not account for the diversity of elements absent from different animals.

Summary

Many of the inferences derived in this section are slightly contrary to our expectations. The groups were not using only the optimal portions of the large animals as expected, but were attempting to retrieve all consumable products. This is apparent from evidence of the return to the site of nearly the entire animal, the processing of nearly all types of long bones for marrow or bone grease, and the boiling of non-marrow-bearing bones with their surrounding meat. The groups may have been operating on a tight scheduling system as well, as implied by the boiling of most food and the absence of meat processing for storage.

Unfortunately the remains of the earlier occupations of Tijeras Canyon at Coconito and Early San Antonio were excluded from the analysis in this section because of an insufficient sample of artiodactyl bones. Most of the periods that were analyzed were those singled out in the previous section on hunting strategies as experiencing possible resource stress. At present it is unknown whether the practices inferred above reflect conditions in all occupations or simply in those under stress.

DISTRIBUTION OF THE FAUNAL REMAINS

Using a computer program designed by Mark Harlan (1979), an attempt was made to discover any variations in the distribution of particular species or types of bone among different areas of the sites (see Phillips, this volume). This type of analysis is exploratory in nature and was begun with few preconceptions of what would be found. The main objective was to aid in evaluating the interpretation of the remains, as the samples we examined each contained different proportions from the total areas sampled, and different proportions of room and trash middens. Any major variations in frequency and number might have biased the results which combined all the deposits. These investigations are not complete, but some preliminary findings are worth noting.

A comparison between room and trash deposits was made to note any significant differences in the relative frequencies of species and body parts represented. Analysis included the San Antonio Middle and Late Middle, and the Tijeras Pueblo Early and Late period remains. No significant differences in the relative proportions of species were found between the trash and room deposits of either site. In the comparison of these deposits only one major pattern was noted; virtually all large mammal body parts, except the foot bones, lower leg, and a few rib fragments, are absent from the rooms. This observation seems to reflect housekeeping. The larger bones would probably have been periodically cleared from the room floors and removed to the trash, while the similar bones of the foot as well as any bones of smaller animals could more easily have sifted into the flooring.

The observation is important for methodological reasons. Even had we not noted earlier that the Coconito remains were primarily from room deposits, the extensive initial processing of large animals could have been inferred from the pattern of body parts present. Of course, we cannot prove that such practices were carried out since the complementary midden deposits were not located during excavation. We did, however, approach the remains with caution so as not to draw possibly erroneous inference.

In comparisons between the trash deposits of the central and the outlying room blocks at Tijeras Pueblo, no significant differences in the representation of species were discerned, nor were any apparent among the various trash middens of San Antonio. No major differences in the body parts were noted either, though these examinations are not yet complete. Since the Tijeras Canyon inhabitants were probably not organized in socially stratified groups, no great variations in the location of preferred species or choice body parts within sites would be expected. Through later investigations, we would like to be able to discern if the pattern of body parts is denser in some trash areas than in other deposits. This might indicate slight differences among the preservation conditions of various areas of the sites. By combining the remains of the faunal deposits, these differences might be masking the effects of decay processes that we attempted to test for. The interpretations of the butchering practices and of the use of particular bones might then be biased.

Very few differences were noted in the species present and the body parts represented among different rooms of each of the three sites, though these examinations are also incomplete. In general, the variations in the composition of the samples from each site and period have not affected the patterns discerned earlier to infer the hunting strategies and the methods of animal processing of the Tijeras Canyon groups.

CONCLUSION

By manipulating the faunal data in various ways, a number of inferences have been drawn concerning the behavior of the canyon communities. These have been summarized at the end of each section. This paper represents an attempt to move away from a simple description of only what faunal remains were found. Such a report would have ended after listing the species and charting their relative frequencies in terms of numbers of bones. Very little would have been learned about the various groups of Tijeras Canyon by stopping there.

The ability to go beyond a purely descriptive level was only accomplished by first establishing a framework within which to examine and compare the remains. The validity of this framework—the assumptions about how human groups behave—is, of course, open to question. Had a different set of assumptions been established, the interpretations would probably have been different. The lack of any explicit framework, however, is at the heart of the problem with many previous faunal reports.

One major benefit of this report is that it offers suggestions concerning specific areas in which further research would be worthwhile. The conclusions should be considered tentative at best, to be re-evaluated at some future time in light of new evidence from the canyon sites and from refinements in the theory and methods of archaeological research.

ACKNOWLEDGMENTS

Thanks to Linda Cordell, who not only persuaded me two years ago that learning to identify animal bones would solve all my problems (and *hers*), but who guided me through much of this analysis. Without her stimulation, evaluation, and patience, many of the ideas in this chapter would never have materialized. Many thanks also to Dana, Yvonne, Emily, Ben, Charlie, Cheryl, and Helene for the interesting discussions we've had over the months in preparing this book, to Wendy Nelson and to the Museum of New Mexico for allowing me to use their material, and to the many archaeologists around the country who have (unknowingly) influenced my thoughts through the publications of their research.

7

Analysis of
Skeletal Remains

Cheryl Ferguson

EDITOR'S INTRODUCTION

The most direct method of interpreting the relationships among the prehistoric peoples of Tijeras Canyon and their relationships with other southwestern groups is to examine the skeletal remains of the people themselves. Ferguson's analysis compares the burial populations of Tijeras Pueblo, Paa-ko, and San Antonio. (Human skeletal remains were not available from Coconito.) Her analyses treat the genetic similarities among these groups and compare them to other southwestern burial populations. She also discusses the paleodemography and paleopathology of the Tijeras populations. Ferguson's paper addresses two important interpretive questions. First, she finds little evidence linking the occupations of Tijeras Canyon genetically to the prehistoric San Juan Basin. Second, she provides some support for the nutritional deficiencies suggested by Young. Finally, her data dramatically remind us how arduous the lives of preindustrial populations are compared to our own.

L. S. C.

> *The skull lay tilted in such a manner that it stared
> up at me as though I, too, were already caught a
> few feet above him in the strata.* (Eiseley 1957)

Bone, as the archaeologist finds it, is but a mineral substance, robbed of the protein-carbohydrate complex that is present during life. It can, however, reveal a great deal of the biology and life-ways of a former people. One may ascertain the sex, age, race, stature, and robusticity of an individual from his skeleton. It is also possible to determine some idea of general health and diet and the presence of certain diseases. Skeletons from a population also provide unique insights into that group's work stresses, and genetic relationships to neighboring peoples.

We know that prehistoric people of the Tijeras area belonged to a widespread group known as the Anasazi, from whom modern Pueblo Indians are descended. Like modern people of the pueblos, they had broad faces, protruding cheek bones, and moderately wide noses. Their hair and complexions were dark, as is evident from naturally preserved mummies found at other sites. The back of Anasazi heads were flattened, for babies were kept in cradle-boards, possibly to increase the freedom of the mother to go about her daily work.

At death, an Anasazi was normally buried with arms and legs flexed, the head pointing eastward. Interments in the Rio Grande area are simple and, unlike the burials of larger pueblos in the San Juan Basin, such as Chaco Canyon, contain few or no artifacts. Some have foodstuffs, presumably to nourish the spirit on its journey. Adults and children are usually found buried just outside the walls of a site, while infants are often found buried beneath the floors of rooms. This practice, common with pueblo infants in the recent past, allowed the baby's spirit to re-enter the mother's womb and be born again as another child (Lange 1968). It appears that burials were sometimes disturbed by the prehistoric Anasazi, as is evidenced by isolated human bones in refuse and fragmentary burials under walls. This means only that the Anasazi view of gravesites was different from our own, not that they had no respect for the dead.

Excavation of a burial requires the greatest of care. Much bone is damaged or missed by the amateur excavator, and myriads of details that can reveal important information to the trained eye are lost. For example, those who are not familiar with the human skeleton often miss many of the smaller hand and foot bones, which can resemble pebbles. Crumbling bone, which cannot survive transportation to a laboratory, can be analyzed on the spot for valuable clues of shape, texture, and size. The precise location of the burial must be noted, position of the body described and sketched to scale, and photographs taken. Then laboratory work involving cleaning, preservation, and inventory must be done before the detailed analysis begins.

THE TIJERAS AREA BURIALS

This study of skeletal material examines burial remains from three sites in the Tijeras area: Tijeras Pueblo, Paa-ko, and San Antonio. Conclusions are made concerning the stature, genetic relationships, demography, and pathology of the canyon people. These conclusions are compared to other Southwest Indian populations both modern and prehistoric. Table 9 describes the samples from each of these sites. The sample sizes vary from site to site and are not as large as could be desired for statistical confidence.

Stature

An individual's stature during life can be estimated from the lengths of his long bones. The anthropologist must be sure, however, that the formulae used for estimation were obtained from a sample of the same racial affiliation as the individual under study, as the body proportions of populations differ. Adequate research with modern Pueblo Indians has not been done, so the statures of prehistoric Tijeras people have been estimated here using formulae derived by Santiago Genoves (1967). Genoves established

TABLE 9. Tijeras Area Burial Sample Sizes

Site	Men	Women	Children 3–18 yrs.	Infants	Total
Tijeras Pueblo	23	19	3	19	64
Paa-ko Pueblo	11	17	11	18	57
San Antonio	9	11	1	7	28
Total	43	47	15	44	149

these formulae by correlating long bone lengths and statures of cadavers selected for their resemblance to pre-Hipanic peoples in Mexico. To assure this, he examined only those with appropriate blood types, ancestors, and gross morphological characteristics, such as hair and eye color, dentition, body hair, skin color, and body form. An example of his formulae, which yields the height of a male, given his femur length, is as follows:

Stature = 2.26 × length of femur + 66.379 ± 3.417 centimeters

Adjustments must then be made to obtain living stature, because cadavers, lying stretched out on a table, are consistently taller than the individuals were in life. Different formulae are used for women and for the various long bones available.

Using these formulae, we find that males in the Tijeras area averaged 161.7 cm (5′5″) and females averaged 151.31 cm (5′½″) in height. The tallest man came from Paa-ko Pueblo and stood 169.0 cm (5′8″). The tallest woman, also from Paa-ko, was 162.0 cm tall (5′5″). The shortest man, 152 cm (5′1″) and the shortest woman, 140.5 cm (4′8″) came from Tijeras Pueblo. Table 10 gives the mean stature, by sex, at each site under study. The only statistically significant difference in stature between sites is that the Paa-koan men were taller than the men of Tijeras. Stature, like most other characteristics, is determined by an interaction between genetic and environmental variables. Of other southwestern sites, Pecos and Pottery Mound most closely resembled Tijeras Pueblo, although Pecos people were very slightly taller and Pottery Mound people slightly shorter (Hooton 1930, Cobb 1978).

To better picture the morphology of Tijeras area peoples, an index was taken on the humerus (bone of the upper arm) to measure robusticity, a characteristic that can indicate work stresses. All three populations were robust, showing that hard work was probably a necessity. Males and females of Tijeras Pueblo show values indicating greater robusticity than their counterparts in Paa-ko, although only the values for females are significantly different

TABLE 10. Mean Stature of Prehistoric Tijeras Peoples (in cm)

	Tijeras Pueblo	Paa-ko	San Antonio
Males	160.13	164.44	162.63
Females	150.35	151.61	153.00

statistically. The San Antonio sample of indices was too small to show reliable results.

Genetic Distance

Differences in skull form or shape between groups reflect, to a large extent, genetic differences between those populations (Howells 1953; Clark 1956; Friedlander 1970). In order to draw conclusions concerning relationships among the various Tijeras area peoples and other populations in the Southwest, these differences in skull form must be quantified. In this study, two types of measurements were taken on each skull complete enough to allow them. First, traditional measurements were made between landmarks on the skull (Figure 44). Second, to elicit subtle differences, a new method of measures was also used (Lumpkin 1976). A trace of the face was overlaid with a grid, and points along the trace were selected (Figure 45). The curvature of the trace was then

45. Trace and grid for facial curvature measurements.

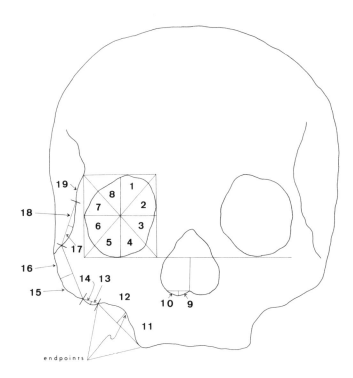

computed for each curve between its end points. These curvatures tell how large a circle with that same curvature is, thus describing the shape of the face better than traditional measures, which describe the face only in terms of dimensions. A computer was used to compare the forty measurements of each skull with the measurements of every other skull, using techniques of multivariate statistics. The computer produced plots to show the relationships that each skull has to all of the others. Separation on the page can be interpreted as genetic distance (Figures 46 and 47). Additionally, a statistic to describe homogeneity (Mahalanobis' D^2) was calculated for each pair of populations. The plot and the statistic were both used to interpret relationships.

The method described here (Lumpkin 1976) is a new one, and can only be applied to crania that are in almost perfect condition. Because these are difficult to find among prehistoric specimens, sample sizes are small. In addition, the tracing of the face, the choice of endpoints for the curvatures, and the fitting of circles to curvatures all depend to some extent on the judgments of a particular investigator, so that data collected by one person may vary slightly from data taken by another. These problems aside, the exercise yielded interesting results. Tijeras and Paa-ko were quite easily separated from each other, implying that those populations are genetically distinguishable (Figure 46). Although there probably was some intermarriage and movement between the two pueblos, group integrity appears to have been maintained. Additionally, the bulk of the Tijeras Pueblo sample, 25–100 years earlier in time than that of Paa-ko, represented earlier generations.

Although Tijeras and Paa-ko are distinguishable, they are more closely related to each other than either is to the southwestern sites of Aztec, Mesa Verde, Pecos, or Pueblo Bonito in Chaco Canyon (Figure 47). The great distance between the two clusters does not support the hypothesis which states that the Tijeras area was populated by people who abandoned the San Juan Basin (Reed 1944, 1949), an idea based upon distribution of pottery types. Further work may well show a closer affinity of Tijeras peoples with Mogollon populations from the south. The present study is but another reminder that distribution of artifact types is not synonymous with movements of people and that, to determine biological relationships, one must study people themselves, rather than the shapes and designs of their tools.

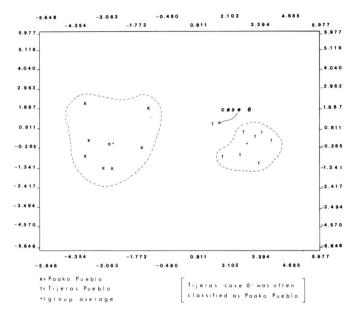

Skattergram: Tijeras Pueblo vs. Paako Pueblo

46. Genetic distance plot of individuals from the Tijeras Canyon sites.

47. Genetic distance plot of individuals from several southwestern archaeological populations.

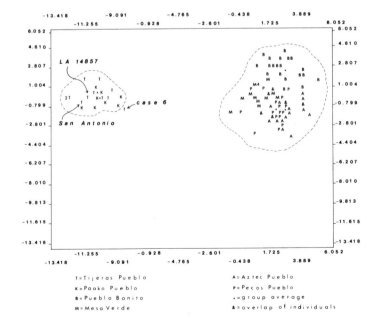

Skattergram: Tijeras Area vs. Northern Pueblos

Only one skull from San Antonio was complete enough to undergo this analysis, a poor sample size to be sure. It was found statistically to resemble most closely those individuals from Tijeras Pueblo. The same is true of the skull of an isolated burial from LA 14857, an outlying site to the west of Tijeras (Figure 47).

Most interestingly, a Tijeras woman 22 to 24 years of age was often classified by the computer into the Paa-ko group. As Lumpkin (1976) has observed in a similar instance, this partial misclassification may be explained in several ways. First, the woman may have been born at Paa-ko Pueblo and subsequently moved, with or without her consent, to Tijeras Pueblo. In mating or raiding women are often chosen because they resemble the receiving group; this could explain the reason she was sometimes classified into the Paa-ko's group. Second, this female may have been a descendant of a former interpueblo mating (Figure 47, Case 6).

Paleodemography

Demography is the study of the size, distribution, and vital statistics of a population. Reconstructing the demography of a prehistoric population based only on skeletal sampling is difficult, as many workers caution (Angel 1969; Ubelaker 1974; Weiss 1976). Because of partial excavation and weathering, anthropologists rarely have the skeletons of all the people from a site. The size of the population must be estimated from indirect evidence such as number of rooms and the size of trash areas. Since the dead are buried in strata other than the ones in which they lived, skeletons are difficult to date. The skeletal population, then, usually represents a considerable time span, including many generations, making interpretations of a restricted point in time difficult. Accurate determination of sex and especially age is somewhat limited by problems of method. At present it is impossible to determine the age of an adult to within three years, and such accuracy is needed for meaningful demographic reconstructions. Finally, the anthropologist must assume similarities between the behavior patterns of past and present populations with similar environments and means of survival. Skeletal analysis can then tell us whether our prehistoric population appears to follow the same patterns, allowing an inference that the processes present in cultures today were also present in the prehistoric one.

Direct skeletal analysis suggests that Tijeras people lived rather short lives, and that adult males, living to about thirty-five years of age, on the average outlived women, who died around thirty-two years of age. This life span is comparable to that found at an Arizona site (Grasshopper), in which males lived to thirty-seven years of age and women lived to be thirty-four years, on the average (Longacre 1976). By contrast, in the United States in 1975, Caucasian males lived, on the average, to be sixty-nine years of age, while women lived to be seventy-seven years old (Public Health Service 1975). The age at death in the Tijeras area (and most other primitive cultures) was probably lower for women because of trauma associated with childbirth.

Infant mortality in the canyon area was high. Approximately 30 percent of the population died under the age of three years. This is a higher death rate than the 23 percent found at the Dickson Mound site, (A.D. 700–1350) in Indiana and the 24 percent found at one Arizona site, Point of Pines (A.D. 1000–1450) (Clarke 1977), but lower than the 50 percent found at the Grasshopper site (A.D. 1275–1400) (Longacre 1976). It is interesting to note that the mortality of nonadults in Tijeras Canyon was highest in the newborn-to-three-year range—the time period preceding and during weaning. It has been suggested (Clark 1977) that the post-weaning period is the one most susceptible to stress, because anemias, parasitic infection, and weanling diarrhea from bacterial contamination of food are worst as the infant moves from its mother's breast to a diet obtained externally. From this suggestion, one would expect mortality to be greatest in the two-to-six-year age group, an expectation which the Tijeras data do not support. Unless weaning was accomplished early, between the ages of one and three, we must look elsewhere for causes of infant mortality. Perhaps mothers were unhealthy, unable to provide the nutrients needed by the infant. In the Tijeras region, it appears that a major cause of infant death was a deficiency, in iron (discussed later).

Such information on mortality can provide a general view of health, as adult longevity is the best single measure of adult health and infant mortality is an indicator of female health stresses. In other words, many deaths mean much illness (Angel 1969; Howell 1973). Prehistoric people in the Tijeras area, then, suffered a great deal of ill health. In this light, it is interesting to look at each of the

three sites separately. Table 11 and Figure 48 provide the percentage of deaths by age group.

The difference between average adult age at death at San Antonio and at Tijeras Pueblo is not significant, but the difference between Paa-ko and both the other pueblos is. People were living
longer on the average at Paa-ko than at the other two Tijeras area

TABLE 11. Percentage of Deaths by Age Among Prehistoric Tijeras Peoples

	San Antonio	Tijeras Pueblo	Paa-ko
Infants 0–3	25.0%	29.7%	31.6%
Children 4–17	3.6%	4.7%	19.3%
Adults 18–30	35.7%	23.4%	14.0%
Adults 31–40	17.8%	26.6%	8.8%
Adults over 40	17.9%	15.6%	26.3%
Total	100.0%	100.0%	100.0%
Average age of adults at death	31.4	32.4	37.6
Average age of infants at death	1.25	1.84	1.61

48. Percentage of deaths by age group for Tijeras area.

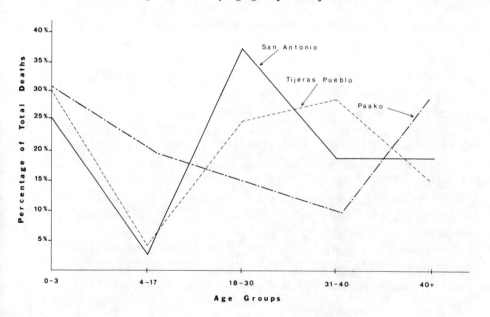

sites. This is contrary to the expected situation, since Paa-ko has the highest infant and child mortality of any pueblo. Assuming the results are not due to sampling error, it appears that Paa-koan people, if they could survive a difficult childhood, had a better chance of living to old age than did other people of the area.

Paleopathology

Paleopathology is the study of disease in earlier human populations. It provides information on the health status of those populations and, because of the relationships of the human body to its environment, can allow inferences concerning a people's nutrition and life-style. Such post-mortem diagnosis is an ambitious endeavor fated to less than complete success, for a skeletal population possesses none of the soft tissues that surround the bony framework during life. Diseases of the intestines, lungs, kidneys, and heart, for example, remain largely unknown. Additionally, the diseases that do affect bone are more difficult to diagnose without knowledge of that malady's effects on surrounding soft tissue. Erosion from soil movement and pressure, groundwater percolation, bacterial action, and rodent activity also impede analysis by destroying bone or by altering its appearance, at times even imitating disease processes. The resulting health picture, gleaned from the incomplete leavings, is therefore only a partial one. Further practical difficulties are encountered, as anthropological laboratories are not often equipped with the precision medical equipment (X rays, densitometers, histological sectioning and staining equipment, and biochemical test facilities) that helps modern physicians make diagnoses.

The pathology found in the Tijeras area has been grouped by etiology (causation) into disturbances of metabolism and nutrition (Table 12), trauma (Table 13), degenerative processes (Table 14), disturbances of prenatal origin (Table 15), infections, vascular problems, and tumor and tumorlike processes. Dental problems are considered separately.

Disturbances of metabolism and nutrition. Such disturbances include dietary excesses or deficiencies. Starvation is often difficult to evaluate in skeletal remains only, for bone usually receives needed nutrients at the expense of depleting fat stores and muscle mass. (Starving persons are often described as being "skin and bones.") By contrast, specific isolated excesses or deficiencies can sometimes be detected in bones. Excessive heavy metals are stored in bone and can be detected grossly or in X rays. Isolated vitamin deficiencies cause symptoms that often are identifiable, although one deficiency may mimic another, making diagnosis difficult. Scurvy is the result of vitamin C deficiency; rickets and osteomalacia (the adult form of rickets) are caused by a lack of vitamin D. Several vitamin deficiencies, however, are often found in one individual, for a poor diet is rarely selectively deficient.

Only one possible cause of vitamin D insufficiency was found in a nine-year-old child from Tijeras Pueblo. A similar lack of rickets and osteomalacia is noted in other studies of the Southwest (Hrdlička 1908; Hooton 1930; Miles 1975).

Porotic hyperostosis is a descriptive term for a disturbance that produces a thickening of the skull and small holes, giving bone an appearance like coral. Although there is debate among scholars, iron deficiency anemia appears to be a likely cause of porotic hyperostosis in the Southwest (El-Najjar et al. 1976a, 1976b; Kuntz and Euler 1972). As iron stores become low, the bone marrow space becomes larger in order to increase production of red blood cells. Simultaneously, the outer, dense table of bone thins and may in time be destroyed, the first evidence of which is the appearance of small pits (Figures 49 and 50). Tijeras area individuals with these cranial lesions were also found to possess pitting elsewhere in the body (in the long bone shafts, scapulae, and calcanea), a condition apparently not reported elsewhere. It appears that postcranial bones are also undergoing an enlargement of marrow space in order to meet the demand for red blood cells.

Iron deficiency anemia was common in the Tijeras area and, in conjunction with diarrhea, was probably a leading contributor to deaths in children and infants (Table 12). Iron deficiency is found throughout the world, but certain groups are more likely to develop it than others: young children with increased iron needs; and women of childbearing age, with loss of iron through menstruation and increased need with pregnancy and lactation (El-Najjar et al. 1976a, 1976b). The unusually high rate of death in the first to third years in the Tijeras area may be the result of prolonged breast-feeding without supplemental iron when the mother's iron stores are low.

To understand the occurrence of iron deficiency, we can look at the Tijeras diet. The iron content of maize, a staple in the area, is

TABLE 12. Disturbances of Metabolism, Prehistoric Tijeras

| | Porotic Hyperostosis | | Wedge Fractures | |
	n	% of total	n	% of adults
Paa-ko infants	14	77.8%	–	———
children	5	45.5%	–	———
adults	0	———	4	14.3%
Tijeras Pueblo				
infants	3	15.8%	–	———
children	0	———	–	———
adults	0	———	5	11.9%
San Antonio				
infants	4	57.1%	–	———
children	1	100.0%	–	———
adults	3	15.0%	2	10.0%

49. 50. Examples of porotic hyperostosis on the upper (Fig. 49) and rear (Fig. 50) skull vault of a child. Note apertures and coral appearance of affected patches. This malady was probably caused by an iron deficiency.

49.

50.

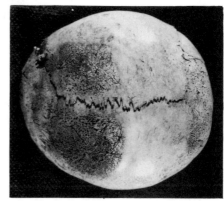

relatively low, and less than 5 percent of it is absorbed by the human body. Additionally, phytic acid, present in all varieties of maize and other plants, inhibits the absorption of iron even if the iron is present from other sources. Animal iron is more readily absorbed and used (El-Najjar et al. 1976b). A population subsisting on a maize and other vegetable diet, with little or no animal protein, is critically and chronically short of iron. Other pueblos that relied heavily on maize and other plants, occasionally supplemented by game, also show a high occurrence of iron deficiency. These include Chaco Canyon in New Mexico and Canyon de Chelly and Inscription House in Arizona. Sites with abundant game animals, however, such as Gran Quivira and the Navajo Reservoir sites in New Mexico, show less porotic hyperostosis (El-Najjar et al. 1976b). Pecos Pueblo, on the edge of a plain suited for hunting, likewise shows a smaller percentage of the disease (Hooton 1930).

In osteoporosis, which is common today, bone becomes porous and structurally weak with the hormonal changes of aging. Everyday stresses can therefore produce considerable skeletal damage. Vertebral bodies often collapse (anterior wedge fracture), causing a spinal curve to the front, which is often seen as a hunchback in elderly women. Anterior wedge fractures from the Tijeras area are summarized in Table 12. All of them were found in people over 40 years of age, but none were so severe as to produce neural damage.

Trauma. This category includes bone fractures, joint dislocations, muscle strains, and sprains of ligaments and tendons. Since all soft tissues have disintegrated, it is difficult to know precisely how traumatic life was for Tijeras area populations, but this study provides no support for the popular notion that these prehistoric people suffered repeated injury and were left maimed and crippled (Table 13).

Foot injuries were a common type of trauma. Blows to the foot (especially the toes) were evidenced in five people from Paa-ko and four from Tijeras Pueblo. This is not surprising, for soft and open sandals provide little protection.

One severe hand injury occurred in a young adult female from Paa-ko. Fusion of two bones of a finger (proximal and middle phalanges) followed a fracture apparently caused by a blow to the slightly bent digit. No movement at the joint was possible following fusion at an angle of 13 degrees.

Three men, one from each site under study, suffered muscle strain and bleeding of the muscles of the interior thigh, causing the tendons to harden into bone material (ossification). Although pain may have been severe at the time of injury, ossification itself produced little discomfort, but the muscles were probably never again as strong as they had been. It is interesting that all three injuries occurred to males over thirty-five years of age, possibly indicating an activity common to this sex (and age?) group, or to a specialized subset of it—for example, professionals in a specific job activity such as the use of a digging stick in crop cultivation or the quarrying of clay. A blow to the muscles or overstretching could also cause this condition.

Evidence of damage to the spine existed in eight cases. Such damage in older people can be the result either of major trauma or repeated small stresses from work such as lifting and carrying of loads, especially on the head. Injury in younger people, however, usually indicates a more severe accident. Pain is present in both cases. Two people over 40 years of age from Paa-ko and an elderly (60+) man from San Antonio suffered neck injury. There were three cases of injury to vertebrae of the trunk; two of these, in men from Tijeras Pueblo and Paa-ko, resulted in slight side-to-side curvatures of the spine. A young Tijeras Pueblo woman showed damage to two discs of the middle back. Lower back injury occurred in a young Paa-koan male and a 24-year-old San Antonio female.

Only one possible cause of traumatic joint dislocation was found, in a hip from Paa-ko. The problem was evidently corrected

TABLE 13. Trauma Among Prehistoric Tijeras Residents

	Tijeras Pueblo	Paa-ko	San Antonio
Foot injury	4	5	0
Adductor muscle strain	1	1	1
Damaged vertebrae			
Neck	0	2	1
Thorax	2	1	0
Lower back	0	1	1
Skull vault injury	1	2	2
Noncranial fractures	4	3	1
Parturition Scars			
Number	6	5	3
Percentage of women	32%	29%	27%

soon after occurrence, causing no physical disability. This man also probably suffered from a painful right elbow, either as a result of a blow, or chronic stress from hard work. The joint cartilage had degenerated extensively for a man of this age (30 to 40 years).

Blows to the skull vault, whether intentional or accidental, were evidenced in five individuals—two from Paa-ko (a female, 30 to 35 years, and a male, 12 to 14 years), one from Tijeras Pueblo (male, 25 to 28 years), and two from San Antonio (infant, 9 months to one year; female, 18 to 21 years). A broken nose was seen in a female, 25 to 30 years old, from Tijeras Pueblo. All these injuries (4.1 percent of the total sample) were healed or healing at the time of death.

Noncranial fractures were limited to eight individuals (5.4 percent) among the three sites. A Paa-koan woman of approximately 45 years had suffered a severe blow from behind to the left elbow. Both the upper arm and one of the forearm bones were broken and dislocated, limiting extension of the elbow to 90 degrees, undoubtedly a bothersome disability. Pain at the time of the incident was surely excruciating.

A blow to the right clavicle (collarbone) in another Paa-koan woman caused a fracture in which the two portions were separated. They never reunited, and the outer end of the damaged bone was progressively resorbed. It had literally disappeared years before the woman died at about 40 years of age.

The most extensive series of fractures were seen in a Paa-koan woman aged about 45 years. We know that she lived for some while after the incident, for healing is complete. In a terrible fall or fight, she broke her right ilium (hip bone), displacing a large portion of the bone. At least two ribs on the left side were broken but healed well. One of her left forearm bones (radius) was fractured near the wrist. This type of fracture (Colles fracture) is often seen in people who have attempted to break a fall with their arms. The radius was displaced slightly but healed. Her neck was also injured, and the woman's jaw was dislocated to the left and front, making chewing difficult. Degenerative arthritic changes were accelerated in joints near the injured parts, causing chronic pain thereafter in her jaw, hip, wrists, and neck. She also suffered from painful arthritic changes, not necessarily related to the accident, in her knees, shoulders, elbows, feet, hands, and back. She could not have survived the trauma had she not been cared for during a long recuperative period.

A male skeleton from Tijeras Pueblo, 40 to 45 years old at death, shows evidence of a healed break with some displacement in the left radius near the wrist, another Colles fracture. Because the corresponding ulna was then slightly longer than this broken radius, there was tension on the joint capsule, resulting in arthritis in this wrist. Pain of movement was probably considerable. As mentioned earlier, this type of fracture is typical as an individual attempts to stop a fall with extended arms.

A third healed break of the radius is seen in a Tijeras Pueblo man 22 to 26 years old. This man also suffered a considerable blow to the right tibia (bone of the lower leg) which, although causing no fracture, resulted in a "bone bruise," painful but not debilitating.

A spiral fracture of the tibia healed in alignment in another Tijeras Pueblo man 30 to 35 years old, but partial bone growth into a muscle and membrane occurred, limiting movement of the knee. Such a spiral fracture is the result of torsional forces, as in a twisted fall where the ankle remains stationary.

A woman of 30 to 35 years from Tijeras Pueblo probably broke the radius in both arms, above the wrists. The accident occurred at a young age, while the bones were still growing. Fracture at such a time will often cause a bone to grow longer than than it would have normally. In this case each radius "overgrew" the other forearm bone, limiting rotation of the wrist to about one-third of its normal mobility and hastening the development of arthritis in that joint.

Only one fracture was evident at San Antonio. A female 30 to 40 years of age shows a completely healed right rib fracture with very little displacement. Comparable numbers of fractures were found in Mesa Verde (Miles 1975), Pottery Mound (Cobb 1978), and Pecos Pueblo (Hooton 1930). It is significant that none of the fractures in any sites mentioned here could be confidently attributed to warfare, although skull fractures might be indicative of violence.

Giving birth, as many women know, has its own element of physical trauma. Some of this injury can be seen in bones of the pelvis. As the fetus develops, ligaments joining the two halves of the pelvis (in front) may be pulled to the point of light bleeding,

leaving permanent pits or grooves on the bone. The presence of
these pits or grooves indicate that the woman has borne at least
one child (Stewart 1957). This principle does not, however, work
in reverse. That is, absence of these pits or grooves does not
necessarily mean that the individual has not borne children, for
different individuals suffer different amounts of damage, depending upon body size, fetus size, shape of the pelvis, and type of
obstetrical practices. Twenty-nine percent of Paa-koan women
showed these "parturition scars," while 27 percent of women
from San Antonio and 32 percent of women from Tijeras Pueblo
exhibited them (Table 13).

Degenerative processes. Diseases of degeneration are a result of
the aging process, which proceeds at different rates in different individuals. Osteoarthritis results when a joint deteriorates and a
bone attempts repair by proliferation. Varying from small osteo-
phytes (boney spurs) to large bridges across joints, it causes pain
and stiffness, but rarely disables, unless joint cartilage degenerates
to the point that one bone makes direct contact with other bones of
the joint. In such a case, movement is so painful that the affected
individual limits it consciously. Joints between vertebrae of the
spine (Figure 51) are the most commonly involved, but other joints

51. Osteoarthritis of four vertebrae. Note proliferating bony spurs,
reaching across the joints, causing some pain and limitation of movement.

(knees, elbows, shoulders, hips, wrists) may also be affected (Figure 52). The incidence of this disease is high in the prehistoric Tijeras area, and it occurs at an earlier age (as early as 30) than in modern Americans. This is true of most prehistoric sites in the Southwest. A Tijeras man of approximately 45 years shows such a fusion of at least the bottom four vertebrae (Figure 51). (He suffered also from extensive degenerative arthritis in his other joints). Table 14 summarizes incidence of the affliction in the Tijeras area.

Paa-ko shows the highest percentage of arthritis, especially in the joints. It is difficult to say at this point whether work stresses were more severe there, or whether the people were predisposed to it biologically. The high incidence of osteoarthritis in these individuals is interesting, for many people believe that such arthritis affects mostly people living in cold and damp climates, and that warm, dry climates discourage the disease. Statistics of Tijeras populations indicate that warm, dry climates do not decrease the

52. Normal knee joint (top) compared with osteoarthritic knee (bottom) of an elderly Tijeras Pueblo woman. Each bone on the left is a femur (thigh), and each on the right is a tibia (calf). Arrow notes proliferation of bone. There is arthritic pitting on the bone surface, but much of the roughness is due to soil and water erosion.

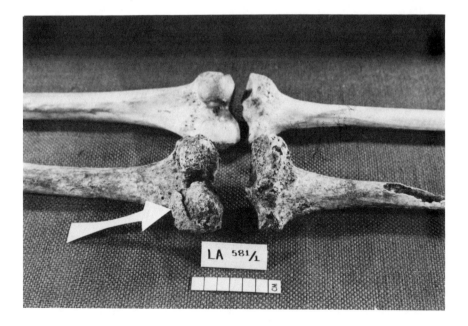

incidence of degenerative arthritis, although they may decrease the symptoms produced by it.

Two individuals (2.2 percent of adults), one from Paa-ko and one from Tijeras Pueblo, show bilateral degenerative changes in the great toes of a type usually associated with bursitis and bunion formation. Bunions have also been found in the Mesa Verde (Miles 1975) and Pottery Mound (Cobb 1978) populations. This is an interesting situation. Narrow, pointed shoes are often implicated in the formation of bunions in present-day peoples, but prehistoric Indians did not possess such footwear. Perhaps bunions are partially genetic in origin, thus varying in frequency from one population to the next. Perhaps travel over rugged terrain increases the incidence. Mesa Verde people, who constantly moved up and down steep canyon walls, do have the highest reported occurrence of bunions.

Disturbances of prenatal origin. Prenatal disturbances are those present from birth. Congenital dislocation of the hip (in which the head of the thigh bone is dislocated from the hip socket, causing a limp) is an interesting malady to examine in the Tijeras populations, as its prevalence is high in a number of present-day Indian groups. Incidence in Navajos varies from 3.05 percent to 3.3 percent (Krause and Schwartzmann 1957; Rabin et al. 1965). Indian inhabitants of Island Lake, Manitoba, have an extremely high incidence of 29.4 percent (Walker 1977), approximately thirty times the incidence in other populations.

Interestingly, no examples of dislocation were found in the Tijeras area, but many instances of anatomical characteristics believed to predispose the hip joint to dislocation do exist. Given the high incidence of congenital dislocation of the hip in modern Navajos, it is not surprising that the highest occurrence of dislocation-related characteristics is found at San Antonio, the only pueblo to yield skeletons from a later period, in which gene mixture from Navajo newcomers is most possible. Such data can

TABLE 14. Degenerative Processes, Prehistoric Tijeras

	Osteoarthritis-Vertebral		Osteoarthritis-Joints	
	n	*% of adults*	*n*	*% of adults*
Tijeras Pueblo	29	69%	15	36%
Paa-ko	20	71%	17	61%
San Antonio	9	45%	6	30%

be useful clinically in testing present-day theories of the cause of congenital hip dislocation. Cradleboards, for example, are often cited as a contributory cause of hip dislocation in children. In the Tijeras populations, however, there is no sign of the disorder in spite of the consistent use of cradleboards inferred from flattened crania. The hypothesis is not supported in this case.

Tijeras area pueblos show a high percentage of spina bifida occulta (Table 15), a condition in which vertebrae (especially of the lower back) fail to form a complete ring surrounding and protecting the nerve centers. It usually does not affect the health.

Anomalies, or atypical characteristics, often occur in individuals without resulting in any noticeable disorder. Since most of them are genetic and occur in most prehistoric and modern populations to a greater or lesser extent, their frequencies are potentially useful in the study of biological relationships between groups. Only a few will be mentioned here. One such anomalous characteristic is "bipartite patellae" in which the patella (kneecap) develops from two centers of ossification (bone formation), rather than the usual one (Miles 1975). If the two centers fail to fuse, the bone develops with a notch in the upper, outer border (Figure 53). Table 15 shows differences in occurrence among the

53. Normal patella, or kneecap (right), compared with a bipartite patella (left), a genetic abnormality in which the bone develops with a notch in the upper border. There is no physical disability in the living person. Differences of patella size reflect different body sizes.

sites, demonstrating nicely the potential of such characteristics in genetic distance studies.

As with modern populations, prehistoric peoples sometimes did not erupt their third molars (wisdom teeth). This noneruption occurred in 10.7 percent of Paa-ko, 21.4 percent of Tijeras Pueblo, and 10.0 percent of San Antonio adults. By comparison, these teeth do not erupt in 13 percent of modern American Indians and in 19.7 percent of American whites (Bass 1971). The especially high number of people in Tijeras Pueblo without wisdom teeth may indicate genetic differences denoting some cultural separation of that pueblo from others in the area. As seen in the earlier discussion of genetic distance, this pueblo is indeed distinguishable from the Paa-ko site.

One adult female over 45 years of age from Paa-ko possesses an extra articulating facet on the right side of the sacrum (pelvis bone). Such an additional set of facets actually provides greater stability than the normal articulation of most spines, but it is unusual. A similar anomaly is exhibited by a male from Paa-ko over 35 years of age. The last vertebra is fused on one side to the underlying sacrum, possibly lessening mobility slightly, but simultaneously increasing stability of the back.

Scoliosis is a side-to-side curvature of the vertebral column. It can be congenital or can result from injury, or disease. If not too severe, it will not inhibit movement. Four instances of probable congenital scoliosis, none severe, were found in the Tijeras area (Table 15). In two of those people, curvature of the back was probably minimal, for the pelvis tipped to one side, taking up most of the deformity. The other two show an S curve of the back. One of these, a forty-five-year-old man from Tijeras Pueblo, possessed a right leg that was shorter than the left. Although the difference is not great, the right leg may have taken more stress than the left, a possibility supported by greater degenerative changes in the right

TABLE 15. Disturbances of Prenatal Origin, Prehistoric Southwest

	Sacral Spina Bifida		Bipartite Patellae		Congenital Scoliosis	
	n	% of total	n	% of adults	n	% of adults
Tijeras Pueblo	5	7.8%	5	11.9%	3	7.1%
Paa-ko	3	5.4%	6	21.4%	1	3.6%
San Antonio	4	14.3%	3	15.0%	0	———
Mesa Verde	–	———	–	5.8%	–	———
Pottery Mound	–	———	–	29.3%	–	———

knee and a larger femoral head on that side. In order to keep the upper body vertical, the spine accommodated by curvature to the left in the lower back and to the right in the upper back.

Infection. Infecting organisms are of many types and can enter the skeleton from the external environment through an open fracture, or from the blood stream. Three instances of infection were found in the Tijeras sample, all in people over 40 years of age. A Paa-koan woman had infections in both tibiae. Her infection was probably hematogenous (blood-borne), since it affected both sides and showed no sign of fracture or laceration. A male, also from Paa-ko, suffered an infection in a toe of the left foot severe enough to produce a sinus in the bone to drain away pus. This infection could have been exogenous in nature for, although no sign of a fracture is evident, a nearby bone shows growth of the sort associated with injury. The best example of a severe infection comes from Tijeras Pueblo. The left femur of this man shows several sinuses near the knee, indicating an abcess in the marrow canal, and surface inflammation (Figure 54). Such an infection

54. Infected femur (top) compared with normal femur (bottom). Note hole for drainage of fluids and lacy proliferation of bone on the surface. This Tijeras Pueblo man suffered acute and chronic pain from this infection, which could have been the cause of his death.

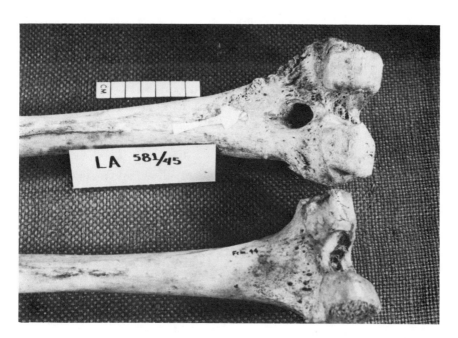

would produce an acute and chronic pain and may have been the cause of death. The invading organisms were probably blood-borne.

Syphilis is an infectious disease. Theories as to its origin abound. Many maintain that the crew of Christopher Columbus carried syphilis to Europe from the New World in 1493. Others believe that syphilis was present in Europe long before this time but was not distinguishable from a number of other diseases grouped under the term "leprosy" (Steinbock 1976). The Tijeras study provided no firm evidence for the pre-Columbian existence of syphilis in the New World, but one Tijeras Pueblo woman over 40 years of age suffered from a disease the effects of which resemble syphilis. It produced destructive lesions on the forehead and nasal area. Arthritic changes are extensive in joints of the spine, shoulders, elbows, wrists, hips, knees, hands, and feet. Additionally, the tibiae show a thickening next to the shin, which resembles the "saber-shin" of syphilitics. There is no evidence in the Tijeras area, however, of congenital syphilis, which should appear were the disease common. Pre-Columbian syphilis has been reported elsewhere in the New World though, at Pecos Pueblo in New Mexico, Indian Knoll in Kentucky, and among the "mound builders" of the Southeast United States, the Aztecs of Mexico, and the Incas of Peru (Steinbock 1976). None was found at Mesa Verde (Miles 1975) or at Pottery Mound (Cobb 1978).

No examples of osseus tuberculosis, another infectious disease, were found in the Tijeras area, nor were any cases found in Mesa Verde (Miles 1975) or Pottery Mound (Cobb 1978) peoples. The high susceptibility of Indians to tuberculosis during written history suggests that the disease was introduced by Europeans, for populations tend to reach an equilibrium with their diseases, building a level of immunity to them.

Scholars believe that populations in pre-Columbian America were too small to have supported epidemic infections such as smallpox, measles, tuberculosis, mumps, chickenpox, and cholera. Such an infection could only spread rapidly and immunize the majority of people at a single stroke. However, turkeys, which were a common domesticate, are known to transfer a series of bacterial and viral infections to humans (salmonella, shigella, ornithosis, and brucellosis). Dogs could have transmitted rabies and a variety of parasital and bacterial illnesses (Kunitz and Euler

1972). Malnutrition, of which we have some evidence, lowers resistance to infections, and the degree of cleanliness would have
been a factor in disease. Archival quotes from early Spanish
contacts speak of a great cleanliness in the pueblos (Kunitz and
Euler 1972). We should be suspicious of this source, however,
knowing the level of hygiene in sixteenth and seventeenth century
Europe.

Vascular problems. With disintegration of soft tissues, direct
evidence of vascular diseases (such as arteriosclerosis) would have
disappeared. Bone is dependent upon blood supply for its survival,
and it can give valuable clues as to behavior of nearby blood
vessels. A possible case of avascular necrosis, or death of a portion
of bone resulting from closure of the artery which nourishes it,
was seen in a San Antonio man 40 years of age. A small, oval
lesion (4.2 mm in diameter) occurred in the knee joint. Vessel
closure in this case could be a result of disease or trauma. A
twenty-five-to-thirty-year-old male from Tijeras Pueblo showed a
similar small, oval lesion on a bone of the ankle. This man, however, probably suffered from a much more serious vascular problem, one which could have caused his death. A vertebra in the
small of the back had been eroded during life, showing a considerable concavity of the body and hinting at the presence of an
aneurysm of the aorta. An aneurysm is a blood-filled sac formed
by the weakening of the walls of a blood vessel. It causes an aching
discomfort and threatens death immediately if broken.

Tumors and tumorlike processes. Neoplasm literally means
"new formation" and refers to an abnormal growth, or tumor (the
term "cancer" is often loosely applied). Malignant neoplasms are
often lethal. Benign tumors are not virulent, but many undergo
transformation to malignant ones with time or irritation. Tumors
can originate in soft tissues (carcinomas or sarcomas) and migrate
to bone, or they can arise in bone initially (osteogenic tumors).
Both types can destroy bone.

Ten individuals with various types of tumors were found in the
Tijeras area populations. Seven of these were adults; three were
immature. Three adult skulls from Tijeras Pueblo possessed osteo-
mata, or benign bone tumors causing no discomfort. One of these
individuals possessed a second type of benign tumor, an osteocar-
tilaginous exostosis. It probably interfered with muscle action and
limited the efficiency of the knee of this woman. Such an exostosis

occurred also in the foot of another woman from Tijeras Pueblo. Two men from San Antonio show exostoses near the knee, one of which limited flexion of that joint. Paa-ko Pueblo also yielded a skeleton with this type of tumor, this time limiting movement at the ankle.

All serious cases of tumors were found in infants and children. Possible cancer in a one-year-old infant from Tijeras Pueblo had spread to the skull and ribs (Figure 55). Histiocytosis, a tumor affecting mostly children and adolescents, was possibly manifested in a Paa-koan infant of two and one-half years, who shows lesions and swelling in an arm and a leg. Bone-destroying lesions in the spinal column and femur of a Paa-koan child approximately twelve years of age may also be manifestations of histiocytosis.

In summary, we see that the two cases of tumors in San Antonio (7.1 percent of that sample) were all benign. Tijeras Pueblo, although exhibiting the greatest number of tumors (7.8 percent of that sample), showed only one case of malignant cancer (in an infant), while Paa-ko, with three cases (5.4 percent) had two instances of malignant tumors. The total number of cases at each pueblo is too small to make a statistically significant statement of differential tumor occurrence.

55. Inner skull table (left) and two ribs (right) of a Tijeras Pueblo infant show signs of possible cancer. Note furrowing and pitting from bone-destroying lesions.

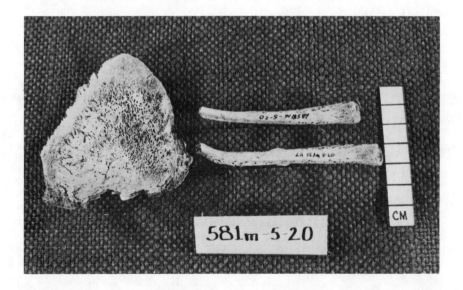

Dental problems. Dental problems abounded in prehistoric individuals. Although tooth decay, or caries, was less common than today, tooth loss was more serious. Southwestern Indians ground corn on stone metates with manos, resulting in meal riddled with sand, which rapidly wore through the chewing surfaces. Forty-seven percent of adults in the area had lost at least one tooth before death, identical to the percentage at Pecos Pueblo (Hooton 1930). Most of them had lost many teeth. Periodontitis, or inflammation of tissues surrounding the teeth, is associated with vitamin C deficiency (Aegerter and Kirkpatrick 1968) and was a common corollary of this dental loss. Caries infected 23 percent of adults, fewer than the 47.9 percent found at Pecos (Hooton 1930), and painful abcesses afflicted 13.3 percent. A single impacted third molar was found at Tijeras Pueblo. This pueblo showed a slightly higher incidence of all dental problems than did either San Antonio or Paa-ko. Possible factors include lower vitamin and fluoride intake from the water supply.

Occasionally, genetic anomalies appear in the mouth. Noneruption of the wisdom teeth was mentioned earlier. A few examples of rotation of teeth in their sockets and additional teeth are seen. Three instances of grooves in the teeth reflect the consistent use of the mouth as a tool by these women, perhaps to moisten and straighten reeds for baskets.

A forty-five-year-old male from Tijeras Pueblo had an interesting dental problem. Before death, he had lost all of his upper teeth and four lower molars, probably as a result of inflammation, the scars of which still can be seen in the jaw. Teeth of the upper left side were lost first (as can be seen by wear patterns), with a resulting restriction of chewing exclusively to the right side. A probable muscle constriction through greater use then worked through time to shift the jaw to that side somewhat and remodel the bone so that it yet sits to the right of midline when articulated with the cranium. As can be seen here, bone is an ever-changing tissue, responding to the stresses put on it.

CONCLUSIONS

It may seem that prehistoric Tijeras populations were relatively healthy, except for nutritional problems. A study of bone, though, can reveal only a portion of the disease pattern present. Their young ages at death reflect the amount and severity of disease that is probably normal for a preindustrial population in equilibrium with its environment. Our modern longevity is unusual, and is due to greatly improved medical knowledge and techniques.

In summary, prehistoric people of the Tijeras area resembled modern Pueblo Indians physically. Average stature for men was 161.7 cm (5′5″), and for women, 151.31 cm (5′5½″). Their everyday lives were probably busy ones, and judging from degree of muscle development and early occurrence of arthritis, they were strenuous. Death came early, and women, because of child-birth complications died at younger ages (32 years on the average) than did men (35 years on the average). They suffered from the same diseases as do many populations today, but their small numbers were probably inadequate to support many epidemics. Nutritional problems related to dependency upon maize resulted in a high infant mortality, most severe at Paa-ko Pueblo.

Multivariate statistical techniques yield data that indicate Tijeras and Paa-ko pueblos to be genetically distinguishable. They are more closely related to each other, however, than either is to the northern pueblos. Information from this study contradicts the hypothesis of settlement of the Tijeras area by peoples from the San Juan region.

ACKNOWLEDGMENTS

Sandra Cobb gave valuable aid in data collection; Charles Sheldon provided photos. I also thank William Milear, M.D., for consultation in different diagnoses, and Stan Rhine, Ph.D., for review for accuracy and editorial changes.

8

Prehistoric Pottery
of Tijeras Canyon

A. Helene Warren

EDITOR'S INTRODUCTION

Compared to skeletal remains, ceramics provide archaeologists with a less reliable source of information about the relationships between and among prehistoric communities and regions. Yet in part because of the durability and ubiquity of potsherds, reconstructions of prehistoric migrations and social interactions are frequently based on ceramics alone. These reconstructions center on interpretations of ceramic types and wares because many anthropologists assume that similarities in design and method of manufacture indicate close social connections among communities. Warren's chapter addresses this assumption. Her work involves using the ceramic types found in the Tijeras sites to provide a general cultural and temporal framework that relates the Tijeras settlements to those of central and western New Mexico. Like Ferguson, she finds little that links the Tijeras sites to those of the San Juan Basin. Warren uses petrographic analysis of the temper found in ceramic vessels made in Tijeras and elsewhere to interpret patterns of interaction and trade as well as to suggest lines of further research. The petrographic data support Young and Ferguson's suggestion that the Tijeras settlements had close ties among themselves.

L. S. C.

Pots and potsherds are invaluable to the prehistorian's efforts to reconstruct the past. Pottery resists decay and can endure for hundreds and even thousands of years. The process of making pottery under primitive conditions is complex and varied in detail from one area to another, although its basic ingredients and methods of manufacture are similar the world over. Clay, the main ingredient of pottery, is one of the most widespread of all mineral resources. Clay can be obtained from shale outcrops of great geologic age, from modern alluvial, lake, or bog deposits, or from decomposed bedrock. Not all clay is plastic and suitable for modeling or firing to the desied hardness, so testing to find a good deposit has always been necessary. Pure clay mixed only with water is generally unsuitable for pottery as it tends to crack and break, and so some other material—rock, sand, crushed potsherds, or organic fibers—is added to temper the clay. Temper prevents cracking during the drying processes.

Prehistoric vessels were fashioned in many ways. Some were modeled from a plastic lump of clay, others were built with coils or filets of clay, yet others were molded in or over various types of forms. The potter's wheel was unknown in prehistoric America, but Southwestern Indian potters often turned the vessel they were making by placing it inside a shallow bowl or "puki."

Vessel surfaces, finished in different ways, might be rough and unpolished, smoothed, or highly polished (Figure 56). At times a thin coat of clay, called a slip, was added to give the surface a special color (Figure 55). If a painted design were to be added, the surface was almost always polished with a hard, smooth tool. Organic and mineral pigments used by potters include carbon black, iron oxides, iron manganese, clay paint, and glaze. Pots may have been fired in pits dug in the ground or above ground with fuel stacked around the pots. Juniper wood was a common fuel in the American Southwest.

Archaeologists discovered many years ago that early potters followed certain traditions in making their vessels and that these traditions changed over time. As an aid to dating sites, the dif-

56. Vessels with different surface finishes. Culinary vessel (left) is scraped smooth. Bowl (right) is slipped, painted, and polished.

ferent traditions in southwestern ceramics have been named and described, and ordered in chronological classifications. Ceramics are classified by examining a series of attributes such as paste color, paint color, temper type, design motif, and, in some cases, the form of the rim. Since ceramic traditions changed through the years, these changes can be arranged in chronological order through stratigraphy or seriation and dated when tree-ring or other measured dates are available.

Ceramic classification in the southwest has been pursued by scholars for more than half a century. In 1916, N. C. Nelson excavated a stratified trash mound at San Cristobal, a large pueblo ruin in the Galisteo Basin. By seriating, or ordering the potsherds level by level, he established the first chronological sequence of pottery types in the Middle Rio Grande Valley. Since then, archaeologists have named, described, and dated many hundreds of pottery types throughout the Southwest. These studies and the resulting information provide much knowledge about southwestern prehistoric pottery, but because the chronologies include an emphasis on attributes that show changes through time, they omit those attributes that can show the place of manufacture.

Identification of the centers of production of ceramics reveals a type of information different from the temporal data of ceramic chronologies. From this information we can begin to understand something about the interaction of different groups in the Southwest. Patterns of trade can be discerned and possibly an understanding of the ties among groups. Using the traditional temporal outline established by southwestern ceramic chronologies, this paper examines the temper of the ceramic assemblages from Tijeras Canyon sites. Efforts are made to determine the source area of the materials used, and hence the probable place of manufacture. The data are then used as a framework for developing a larger picture of the social and political interactions among prehistoric southwestern groups in the Rio Grande Valley. For this purpose, the Rio Grande area is subdivided into the upper Rio Grande (north of La Bajada), the lower Rio Grande (south of Socorro), and the middle Rio Grande (between the two) (Figure 4). The techniques employed in this study are those developed by earlier researchers examining similar problems.

ANALYTICAL STUDIES OF SOUTHWESTERN CERAMICS

Early in the 1930s, Anna O. Shepard undertook an analytic study of the pottery of Pecos Pueblo in order to learn about the type of materials used and methods of production (Kidder and Shepard 1936). Two primary analytic techniques were used, petrographic analysis of temper and microchemical analysis of glaze paint. Although many other analytic methods have been proposed and used in quantitative studies of ceramic methods, the petrographic microscope is considered the most effective tool devised thus far (Matson 1960). The microscope is used to identify minerals and other aplastic inclusions that were used to temper the clay (Figure 57).

Because the sources of different materials suitable for temper are not evenly distributed throughout the Southwest, petrographic studies can be applied to larger archaeological problems such as the identification of centers of production and the direction and volume of trade. The origins and diffusion of ceramic traits may also be investigated, and refinements of ceramic classification and chronologies and establishment of local sequences of pottery types may result. As studies progress, ceramic traits that are reflections

57. Enlarged cross section of a pot sherd showing slip and temper. The slip appears as a thin haze on the upper portion of the sherd. The dark and light granular fragments within the sherd are temper.

of cultural factors may be distinguished from those resulting from the properties of the natural materials used. Perhaps of greatest importance may be the recognition of archaeological problems not suspected from other lines of evidence.

The first and most important result of Shepard's investigations of Pecos pottery was the evidence of extensive trade. Before this study, many archaeologists had assumed that each prehistoric household produced its own pottery for domestic use. By identifying the minerals and rocks that were used to temper the pottery clays, and by locating their geologic sources, Shepard demonstrated that extensive networks in ceramic trade existed during the centuries when Pecos Pueblo was occupied, ca. A.D. 1250–1839. Subsequent studies of ceramics from Petrified Forest in Arizona, showed that pots had been traded widely throughout the Southwest since the first pottery was made in the early centuries A.D. (Shepard 1953).

Shepard's study also showed that stylistic differences in pottery often correlated with temper preferences, helping to explain sudden changes in the appearance of ceramics. For instance, at Pecos Pueblo Shepard (1936) found that a supposedly "degenerate" glaze-paint ware was actually a reflection of the trials and errors of the beginnings of glaze-paint production at the village and not deterioration of a ceramic industry.

Early Archaeological Sites and Associated Pottery in Tijeras Canyon

The earliest pottery found at an archaeological site in Tijeras Canyon belongs to what has been referred to as the San Marcial complex (Mera 1935). In addition to vessels of San Marcial Black-on-white, the assemblage included plain brown ware, highly polished slipped red ware, smudged plain ware, and red-on-terracotta vessels. The San Marcial complex is not well dated in the Rio Grande region, with a single archaeomagnetic date of A.D. 580 (Frisbie 1967). Numerous tree-ring dates for the complex in western New Mexico range from ca. A.D. 500 to 625 (Bannister et al. 1966a, 1966b).

Temper analysis of about seventy-five San Marcial sherds from the type site in central New Mexico showed that over 90 percent contained fragments of hornblende latite from the Datil Volcanics of the Socorro region, indicating local manufacture there. San Marcial sherds with similar temper have been found in the Albuquerque area, suggesting early trade of this ware. The white clay of the San Marcial vessels precludes local manufacture in the Albuquerque area, as no white clays are known to occur there.

The plain wares described by Mera (1935) have since been named Lino Polished, Woodruff Brown, Obelisk Gray, and so on, depending upon the area the wares were found. Polished redwares, or Lino Red, were also made in northern New Mexico, though not necessarily in the Rio Grande area. Archaeologists have referred to the slipped redwares by various names, but Lino Red was the first designation (Wendorf 1953). Redwares imported from southern New Mexico, with rhyolite tuff temper, have been found at sites in the northern Rio Grande, and appear to be in the same tradition as Lino Red. Smudged wares of this early period are probably more common in the west than in the Rio Grande area. The San Marcial ceramics are among the earliest made in the Anasazi region, and were produced throughout western New Mexico, but apparently not in the upper Rio Grande Valley.

Although little is known of subsequent developments of the ceramic industries in the Socorro area, in northwestern New Mexico the successors of the San Marcial wares included White Mound Black-on-white, Kiatuthlanna Black-on white, Red Mesa Black-on-white, Lino Grey, and other utility wares. The black-on-white carbon painted wares found in the Rio Grande are best described for the San Juan Basin, where Piedra Black-on-white and Cortez Black-on-white were counterparts of the mineral painted wares found near Zuni and in the Puerco and Red Mesa valleys. Decorated redwares were made in the Four Corners area. Until about A.D. 1000, these wares were traded to the residents of the Middle and Upper Rio Grande regions. Only utility wares, including such types as Taos Plain and Taos Incised, seem to have been made in the Rio Grande with local rock temper. Potsherds found on campsites or workshop areas at the famous turquoise mines of Cerrillos indicate that the miners were trading for or importing Kiatuthlanna and Red Mesa pots that had been made in western New Mexico. Sherds of similar vessels have been found distributed far out into eastern New Mexico.

The first pottery made in the Rio Grande is thought to be a mineral painted ware called Kwahe'e Black-on-white (Mera 1935). Mera believed that Kwahe'e was a copy of western Cibola or Chaco wares, but Kidder (1936:587) and Gladwin (1945) both saw a resemblance to the pottery of the Four Corners or northern San Juan district. Kwahe'e first appeared around A.D. 1100, about the time another mineral painted type, Socorro Black-on-white, began to appear as an intrusive ware throughout the Rio Grande region. Socorro pottery is indigenous to west central New Mexico—the vicinity of Socorro west to Datil. Associated with Socorro Black-on-white are brown utility wares, often with narrow neckbanding or indented corrugations and contemporary smudged brown ware bowls termed Los Lunas Smudged (Mera 1935). Local copies of these wares were made in Tijeras Canyon and tempered with Precambrian mica schist, which crops out west of Tijeras Pueblo. A similar pattern of ceramic trade from west central New Mexico or Mogollon area can be found in northwestern New Mexico, beginning around A.D. 1100.

Kwahe'e and Socorro pottery were soon followed by the appear-

ance of the first carbon painted ware of the Rio Grande, Santa Fe
Black-on-white, which is reminiscent of similar pottery made in
northwestern New Mexico during the eleventh, twelfth, and thirteenth centuries and found in Chaco Canyon. Santa Fe pottery is
characterized by fine-grained, well-indurated vessel walls, grayish
clay, often with white slipped interiors, and black carbon painted
designs. Other locally made carbon painted wares in the Tijeras
area and throughout the upper middle Rio Grande included Galisteo Black-on-white, which is technologically related to McElmo
Black-on-white of the San Juan region, and a similar, at times indistinguishable, ware which is stylistically akin to Mesa Verde
Black-on-white.

Analysis of the sherds from Tijeras Canyon indicate that potters
used muscovite schist or medium-grained sandstone to temper
their clays. Crushed sherds were also used in decorated wares,
usually mixed with the local rock. The silvery mica schist fragments are quite conspicuous, particularly in the utility or cooking
jars. A variety of tempering materials were noted in the carbon
painted wares, but almost all indicated either local production or
trade from neighboring villages in the Tijeras area.

The black-on-white pottery from Coconito Pueblo was compared to similar wares from Tijeras Pueblo. The temper types of
both decorated and utility wares were identified with a stereomicroscope. The predominant temper class in both samples was
quartz mica schist, mineralogically like the Precambrian schist
which occurs about three miles east of Coconito Pueblo and a mile
or two west of Tijeras Pueblo. The schist can also be found in
channel gravel and terrace deposits along Tijeras Arroyo. Another
outcrop is located near Paa-ko Pueblo, about ten miles north of
Tijeras.

There are some notable differences in temper distributions between the two sites (Warren 1976). At Coconito Pueblo, 67 percent of the utility ware sherds contained mica schist. Welded tuff,
from the Mogollon Mountains, was found in 14 percent of the
Coconito utility sherds, but was absent at Tijeras. This variation
in the pattern of temper distribution could be a result of the sampling procedure used in the study, or it could reflect chronological
differences or cultural preferences. The initial analysis of sherds
from these two sites was not extensive enough to provide a
definitive answer. Recognition of anomalies of this nature,

though, is a step in the process of archaeological research that can give direction to future studies.

The Glaze Paint Pottery of the Rio Grande

The glaze wares were made in the Middle and Upper Rio Grande regions from about A.D. 1315 until the early 1700s (Figures 58, 59). Tijeras Pueblo was built at the beginning of this period. Production of glaze paint ceramics began early in the Tijeras Canyon area. After the founding of Tijeras Pueblo in 1300 the glaze paint wares eclipse the black-on-white wares in frequency. The black-on-white wares are still present in Tijeras Canyon, but they are not as abundant. The classification of the glaze wares was established by Mera in 1933 (Table 16 and Figure 59). Only the red slipped glaze types of Group A have been found at Tijeras.

Until A.D. 1300, or shortly thereafter, Rio Grande potters had been decorating their pots with iron or carbon paint on white or gray surfaces. The ceramic tradition of decorating red-surfaced vessels with black or brown lead glaze paints was a significant departure from the earlier painting techniques. In addition to lead

58. Rio Grande glaze ware. The three sherds are Glaze A. The sherd on the left shows the typical straight A rim. The edges of the sherd on the lower right have been ground.

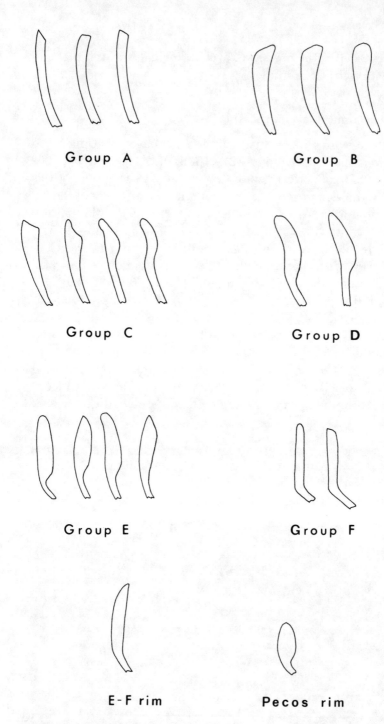

Group A

Group B

Group C

Group D

Group E

Group F

E-F rim

Pecos rim

59. Rim profiles of Rio Grande glaze wares A through F.

glazes, white clay and red matte design elements framed with glaze paint appeared for the first time.

The use of glaze paint was not a completely new technique in the American Southwest, however, as it appears on early black-on-white wares. Dr. Zies of the Carnegie Institution analyzed some Basketmaker II vessels that may date to the sixth or seventh century, from the San Juan area and found them to be decorated with lead glaze (Shepard, 1939:255–58). A black iron silica glaze paint was found on pueblo pottery in the same region, dating to the tenth or eleventh century. Similar black glaze paint occurs on black-on-white vessels dating from A.D. 500 to about A.D. 1400, from the Socorro area west to Quemado, and in eastern Arizona. Glaze paint was used on redwares made in western New Mexico or eastern Arizona at the end of the thirteenth century. Glaze painted pottery has also been reported from northern and western Mexico. But production of glaze paint pottery was sporadic in the American Southwest until the florescence of the Rio Grande glazes after A.D. 1300.

The discovery of lead minerals in the mining district of Cerrillos and possibly other districts, including New Placers, Tijeras, and Socorro, was undoubtedly instrumental in the rapid development

TABLE 16. Classification of Rio Grande Glazes*

Group	Type Name	Estimated Date of Manufacture
pre-A	Los Padillas Glaze Polychrome	?1300 to 1325?
A	Arenal Glaze Polychrome	?1315 to 1350?
	Agua Fria Glaze-on-red	1315 to 1425
	San Clemente Glaze Polychrome	1325 to 1425
	Cieneguilla Glaze-on-yellow, Glaze Polychrome	1325 to 1425
B	Largo Glaze-on-yellow, Glaze Polychrome	1400 to 1450
C	Espinoso Glaze Polychrome	1425 to 1500
	Pottery Mound Glaze Polychrome	1400 to 1490
D	San Lazaro Glaze Polychrome	1490 to 1515
E	Puaray Glaze Polychrome (early)	1515 to 1600
E-F	Puaray Glaze Polychrome (late)	1600 to 1650
E and F	Pecos Glaze Polychrome	1600 to 1700
F	Kotyiti Glaze-on-yellow, Glaze-on-red, Glaze Polychrome	1650 to 1700 or 1750?

*Modified from Mera 1935

of the Rio Grande glaze paint industries. Until recent years, archaeologists had assumed that southwestern Indians had obtained their minerals from surface outcrops, but in 1972 extensive subsurface prehistoric lead mines were discovered in the Cerrillos District. Pottery associated with the mining activities dates from A.D. 1300 to A.D. 1700 (Warren 1969, 1975). The pueblo lead mines were very likely the mines "discovered" by early Spanish explorers during the sixteenth century, and may have provided an incentive for subsequent colonization of New Mexico by the Spanish in A.D. 1598.

The origin of the Rio Grande glaze paint wares has not been determined. The means of transmittal of ceramic traits has been a subject of discussion among archaeologists for nearly a century and the origin of the Rio Grande glazes has received a good share of their attention. Several writers have suggested that the technique of producing glaze paint was derived from the Little Colorado and Zuni regions, in western New Mexico and eastern Arizona (Mera 1935; Shepard 1942; Wendorf and Reed 1955).

Glaze paint red wares appeared in the Little Colorado and Zuni area about A.D. 1290 or earlier and included St. Johns Polychrome and Pinedale Glaze-on-red (Carlson 1961). Heshotauthla Glaze-polychrome, thought to be made in the Zuni area, has been dated between A.D. 1300 and A.D. 1375. At Tijeras Pueblo, Arenal Glaze-polychrome, an early Rio Grande glaze type which may date as early as A.D. 1315, was made in the same decorative tradition as Heshotauthla Polychrome. Agua Fria Glaze-on-red from the middle and northern Rio Grande is most like Pinedale Glaze-on-red, while San Clemente Glaze-polychrome might be considered the Rio Grande glaze counterpart of the type from the Zuni vicinity, Kwakina Polychrome, which was contemporary with Heshotauthla Polychrome.

When two similar wares are as closely dated as the early Rio Grande glazes and the Western glazes, the possibility that the two traditions may have derived from a third source should be considered. Criteria for specifying the means by which pottery styles or techniques were transmitted from one group to another have not been established. Before diffusion or population movement can be inferred, however, identification of the production center of donor groups and associated cultural traits of the potters should be known. Similar data should be sought for the recipient group as well.

The Glaze Paint Wares of the 14th Century

The first glaze paint vessels produced in the Rio Grande region were a heterogeneous group collectively named Los Padillas Glaze-polychrome (Mera 1935). This designation meant only that the pots were made in the Rio Grande area and preceded Agua Fria Glaze-on-red and other Group A types (Table 16).

Arenal Glaze-polychrome (Mera 1935) was named for pottery found near the village of Arenal, south of Albuquerque. It is characterized by a thin line decoration in white clay paint on the exterior of bowls; otherwise, it is indistinguishable from Agua Fria Glaze-on-red, a contemporary type. Arenal is a common glaze paint type at Tijeras Pueblo, and in addition to being tempered with sherd and mica schist fragments, it often has silvery white mica inclusions in the white matte paint.

In 1936, Kidder named and described Heshotauthla Polychrome, a glaze polychrome from the Zuni area, basing the description on sherds similar to those found at Pecos. Some of the Pecos sherds were tempered with "irregular and distorted aggregates of mica, evidently from a schist," and may have been from vessels made in the Tijeras area, where Precambrian mica schist was the common tempering material. Except, perhaps, for the differences in clay or temper, Heshotauthla and Arenal have identical attributes.

Agua Fria Glaze-on-red was by far the most common Group A type of the Rio Grande glazes found at Tijeras Pueblo. Agua Fria is characterized by its polished red slip on jar and bowl exteriors and a glaze paint design; rims are direct, and rounded to squared. Most early Agua Fria generally has sherd temper, but crushed rock was used for temper in some of the very earliest vessels, particularly in the Santo Domingo Valley. San Clemente Glaze polychrome differs from Agua Fria in having a light colored slip on at least one of the bowl surfaces and on part of the exterior of jars. Otherwise, similarities of temper and clay to Agua Fria suggest that San Clemente was made in the same villages, if not by the same potters. Glaze paints ranged in color from black to yellow, brown, or, when misfired, green.

Two other types made during the fourteenth century and belonging to the Glaze A Group, are Cieneguilla Glaze-on-yellow and Cieneguilla Glaze-polychrome (Figure 60). The surface colors of the Cieneguilla vessels range from white to cream or light pink.

Forms are similar to Glaze A red wares, but temper analysis indicated that the Cieneguilla vessels, which were most common in the Galisteo Basin, were made in different villages from the red wares. The Cieneguilla wares were not found at Tijeras Pueblo.

Mineralogical Studies of the Rio Grande Glaze Paint Wares

In conjunction with archaeological excavations in the Cochiti Reservoir area by the Museum of New Mexico in the 1960s, I began mineral or petrographic studies of the Rio Grande glaze paint pottery from the Alfred Herrera Site (LA 6455). The purpose of the study was to obtain information concerning the source materials used in locally made pottery in order to refine local ceramic taxonomy and chronology. Using guidelines suggested by Shepard (1963), about fifteen hundred Group A to Group E glaze rim sherds (Figure 58) were examined with a stereomicroscope, and a framework for pottery class and temper type was established. These temper groups have served as a framework for subse-

60. Cieneguilla Glaze-on-yellow bowl.

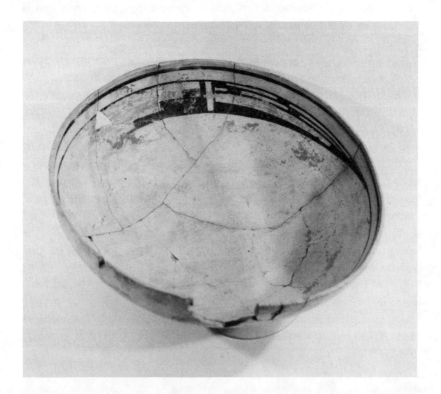

quent studies of the glaze-paint wares in the Upper Middle Rio Grande area (Warren 1968).

A primary result of the Cochiti studies was the identification of manufacture and trade centers during the 400 years that Rio Grande glaze-paint wares were made. Inferences concerning trade centers were based upon the distribution patterns of pottery types within each temper group and time period (Warren 1977). During Group A, A.D. 1315–1425, there were more production centers than in later periods (Table 17). Trade centers included villages in the Galisteo Basin, Cochiti area, at San Felipe, and at Pottery Mound. In addition, many villages were making pottery for local use only, including the Zia villages, Kuaua, and Gipuy.

Some of the earliest glaze tradewares in the Rio Grande were made in the Cochiti and San Felipe area. Between A.D. 1350–1475, San Marcos Pueblo in the Galisteo Basin was the major trading center in the Rio Grande, supplying neighboring villages with vessels of Cieneguilla Glaze-on-yellow and Largo Glaze-on-yellow, mainly. By A.D. 1450, Tonque Pueblo, in the Hagan Basin,

TABLE 17. Major Centers and Periods of Trade of Rio Grande Glazes*

Centers of Trade and Glaze Types	Estimated Period of Trade (A.D.)
San Felipe area (Agua Fria, San Clemente)	1315–1350
(Puaray, Kotyiti)	1600–1680
Albuquerque area ? (Agua Fria, San Clemente)	1315–1350
Cochiti area (Agua Fria, San Clemente)	1315–1400
Pottery Mound (Agua Fria, San Clemente, Pottery Mound Glaze Polychrome)	1315–1490
San Marcos Pueblo (Cieneguilla, Largo, Espinoso)	1350–1475
Misc. Galisteo Pueblos (as above)	1350–1475
Tonque Pueblo (Espinoso, San Lazaro, Puaray)	1425–1550
Abo Pueblo (Agua Fria, Espinoso, San Lazaro, Puaray, Kotyiti)	1350–ca.1675
San Cristobal Pueblo ? (Glazes C to F)	1450?–1680?
San Lazaro Pueblo (Puaray, Kotyiti)	1600?–1680
Pajarito Plateau (Puaray)	1550–1600
Cochiti Pueblo (Puaray, Kotyiti)	1550–1680
Quarai Pueblo (Kotyiti)	1600–ca.1675
Zia Pueblo (Kotyiti)	after 1650
Pecos Pueblo (Pecos Polychrome)	1600–1700
Galisteo Pueblo (late Kotyiti Glaze Polychrome)	1706–?

*Modified after Warren 1970

began to take over the trade industry; to the south, Pottery Mound and Abo Pueblo were the major suppliers of pottery to the Middle Rio Grande villages.

After Spanish explorers and colonists arrived in the Southwest in the sixteenth and seventeenth centuries, ceramic trade centers shifted again. Villages on the Pajarito Plateau, San Lazaro and San Marcos in the Galisteo Basin, and Pecos Pueblo produced pots for export. By the Pueblo Revolt of 1680, the glaze paint industries had virtually disappeared, although the potters of Pecos continued to trade their glaze wares until the turn of the century. After Galisteo Pueblo was resettled in 1706, its potters probably produced a late glaze ware that was widely distributed at least during the early decades of the century. It is not known when the last glaze-paint vessels were made, but Spanish mining activities in the Cerrillos District may have hastened the final disappearance of this ancient ceramic tradition in the early 1700s.

The Glaze Paint Ceramics of Tijeras Canyon

Analysis of ceramics from the Tijeras Canyon sites indicates that the canyon peoples were interacting with other groups in the Rio Grande area. West of Tijeras Canyon and across the Rio Grande were numerous glaze-paint producing villages contemporary with Tijeras Pueblo, including Arenal Pueblo, the type site for Arenal Glaze-polychrome. Most of these villages were abandoned by A.D. 1400 or shortly thereafter.

The ceramic assemblage at San Antonio includes Santa Fe Black-on-white, Galisteo Black-on-white, Wiyo Black-on-gray, Chupadero Black-on-white, St. Johns Polychrome, Los Padillas Glaze-polychrome, and Agua Fria Glaze-on-red. The dates of these ceramics indicate an occupation between A.D. 1200 and A.D. 1375. San Antonio was reoccupied during the late sixteenth and early seventeenth centuries by Pueblo Indians, and during the nineteenth century by Spanish-speaking residents. We are concerned here only with the first occupation.

Heshotauthla, Los Padillas, and Arenal Glaze-polychromes from San Antonio have similar sources of manufacture, according to temper type distribution patterns, to their counterparts found at Tijeras Pueblo. As mentioned before, Arenal Polychrome is a Rio Grande counterpart of Heshotauthla Polychrome. Little is known

of the manufacturing centers or distribution of Heshotauthla Polychrome, although it is reported to be common in the Cibola area
between A.D. 1300 and A.D. 1375 (Carlson 1970:82).

At San Antonio it was assumed that pots with cream-colored
clay and crushed white sherd temper were western imports. This
may be incorrect, for a local or an intermediate source, such as the
Acoma area, is possible. At least 50 percent of the early polychrome glaze wares were tempered, in part, with silvery mica
fragments and angular grains of milky quartz, possibly derived
from the Precambrian mica schist near the village. Sherd samples
were too small to determine if any of the five temper-clay varieties
of mica schist temper were produced at San Antonio.

Agua Fria Glaze-on-red sherds included a wide variety of
temper types, but only about 20 percent contained mica schist. In
contrast, up to 40 percent are tempered with crushed igneous or
volcanic rocks of the Santo Domingo and Galisteo basins. These
include olivine basalt of the Tonque Valley, and augite latite of the
Galisteo Basin. The few Cieneguilla Glaze-on-yellow sherds present at San Antonio indicate trade from San Marcos Pueblo in the
Galisteo Basin, the Cochiti, and the Tonque areas.

The carbon painted wares of San Antonio, contemporary with
early pre–Group A and Group A glaze paint wares, were apparently more abundant than the glazes. Galisteo Black-on-white, as
described by Lambert (1954), is the predominant carbon-paint
ware at San Antonio. The group also includes some of Lambert's
Santa Fe Black-on-white, which has exterior polish and squared
rims, and is technologically similar to the Galisteo wares. About
40 percent of the Galisteo sherds examined at San Antonio contained Precambrian schist fragments and crushed sherd. Sherd
and sandstone temper appears to have been equally common
among the Galisteo wares but are more varied, suggesting these
are imports from other areas.

Two major ceramic traditions have been noted at San Antonio
during its first occupation period, the Galisteo Black-on-white
wares and the early Rio Grande glaze wares. Most archaeologists
suspect that the carbon paint wares derived from the Mesa Verde
area around A.D. 1300, and that the glaze paint wares tradition
stemmed from the west, perhaps the Zuni area, before A.D. 1350
(Lambert 1954:174). At present, there does not seem to be any
significant evidence that one tradition preceded the other at San

Antonio, although there is a general predominance of the carbon-paint wares. This could be a result of cultural rather than temporal factors.

Paa-ko is located about ten miles northeast of Tijeras, and like San Antonio, includes historic as well as prehistoric occupations. The Northeast Communal House was constructed around A.D. 1300 and abandoned by A.D. 1425 (Lambert, 1954). The ratio of glaze paint pottery to carbon paint wares at the Communal House was 48 percent to 52 percent. At Tijeras Pueblo these ratios are reversed (Judge 1974). At Paa-ko, only 6 percent of the glazes were classed as early or transitional, while at Tijeras 20 percent, including Arenal Glaze-polychrome, were early. Only 10 percent of the Agua Fria Glaze-on-red sherds were tempered with mica schist at Paa-ko, although a local source is available immediately north of the Pueblo. One half of the sherds examined were from vessels imported from the Rio Grande villages of San Felipe, Cochiti, Tonque, and possibly Kuaua, and the Galisteo Basin village of San Marcos. As at San Antonio, the carbon painted pottery at Paa-ko bears a strong resemblance to Mesa Verde Black-on-white pottery of the thirteenth century. If found on Chacra Mesa or even along the Rio Puerco in the west, these wares could easily be classified as Mesa Verde Black-on-white.

The ceramic assemblage at Tijeras Pueblo included early transitional or pre–Group A glaze wares, and Group A glazes. Associated with the glaze paint wares are carbon-paint wares including Galisteo, Santa Fe, and Wiyo white wares dating to the thirteenth and fourteenth centuries in the Rio Grande. Of the early transitional glaze types, which constitute nearly 20 percent of the total glaze-paint assemblage at Tijeras, the Heshotauthla, St. Johns, and Kwakina Polychromes found are possible imports from western New Mexico. Los Padillas and Arenal Glaze polychromes were very likely made at Tijeras as nearly 60 percent were tempered with sherd and fragments of Tijeras mica schist.

Agua Fria Glaze-on-red, the most common of the early Group A glazes found here, was also tempered with the local Tijeras schist and crushed sherd in about 50 percent of the sample examined. Trade wares from villages in the San Felipe, Cochiti, and Tonque villages were missing at Tijeras Pueblo, but basalt tempered sherds, possibly from the Albuquerque or Los Lunas area, were noted.

Archaeologists have not found evidence of a time difference between Galisteo Black-on-white and other carbon painted wares, and the early and Group A glaze wares at Tijeras Pueblo. Cordell (1977a) noted that there was no discontinuity in building between A.D. 1200–1325 and A.D. 1325–1600. Throughout the Rio Grande region, many Galisteo Black-on-white villages are associated with the earliest Rio Grande Glaze-paint wares, although other presumably contemporary sites, such as Pueblo del Encierro (LA 70) in the Cochiti area, may lack Galisteo Black-on-white pottery.

CONCLUSIONS

The overall similarities of ceramics important to the temporal chronologies indicate a different sort of interaction than that evidenced by the analysis of temper. By looking at the ceramic types, material used to temper ceramics, their distribution patterns, and by tracing the geographic location of its source, the actual place of manufacture of the ceramics can be identified. From this a specific notion of exchange relations can be developed. The early mineral-painted wares such as San Marcial came into Tijeras Canyon from central New Mexico. Interaction with groups to the south is evidenced by the presence of brownwares from the Socorro area. At San Antonio and Paa-ko, ceramics from the northern villages of Cochiti and San Felipe indicate contact with the upper Rio Grande region. It is interesting to note that most of the trade wares at Tijeras Pueblo appear to come from the west, in the Rio Grande Valley, rather than from closer villages to the north. Some of the imported wares, such as Cieneguilla at San Antonio, are not present at Tijeras Pueblo.

Temper analysis of ceramics can also reveal resemblances in the assemblages which may be indications of overall social and political interactions. Some of the early ceramic assemblages of Paa-ko and San Antonio are tempered with material from the Galisteo Basin. Coconito ceramics indicate ties with the Socorro area. This southern influence seems to be absent at Tijeras Pueblo which was occupied somewhat later. About fifty percent of the ceramics analyzed at Tijeras Pueblo were tempered with local material but resemble the ceramic styles of other areas.

The early Rio Grande carbon paint wares such as Santa Fe Black-on-white can be seen as a counterpart of thirteenth-century wares from the San Juan Basin. Later the influence of Mesa Verde pottery becomes important, as can be seen in the stylistic similarities between Mesa Verde pottery and Rio Grande Galisteo wares. By about A.D. 1300 Heshotauthla-style pots were made at Tijeras Pueblo in the fashion of Zuni ceramics. During the fourteenth century the Rio Grande glazes become the dominant ceramic type. The many different styles of Rio Grande glazes, each from a particular locality—Arenal, Agua Fria, Los Padillas—indicate that the Rio Grande area was not in itself an integrated political unit, but within it were several shifting centers of influence.

9

A Technique of
Ceramic Analysis

Bennie Phillips

EDITOR'S INTRODUCTION

In addition to aiding archaeologists in establishing the temporal and social provenience of their sites within a regional context, ceramics are widely used to interpret chronological position and social relationships within a single site. When ceramic types, rather than attributes, are used as the basis for these interpretations, archaeologists are making several assumptions. These include assuming that types follow a normal curve in popularity over time and that types represent ideas shared about ceramics that vary regularly with social distance. When these interpretations are applied to deposits in sites that by their very nature offer poor temporal and spatial control, the assumptions multiply. Trash deposits that are spatially separated from rooms and activity areas are prime examples of situations where temporal and spatial control are at a minimum if fine grained ordering is desired. Phillips' paper discusses some of the reasons why secondary trash deposits are difficult to interpret. He introduces a technique of analysis that minimizes error and applies the technique to the trash at Tijeras Pueblo. Importantly, the technique is

confirmed by data from the same site that are independent of
ceramics.

L. S. C.

————————◆◆————————

This analysis of the ceramic assemblage recovered from the
trash dumps at Tijeras Pueblo had two objectives. The first was to
see if changes in ceramic types recovered from the trash deposits
could be used to separate different occupational episodes when no
other stratigraphic data were available. The ability to distinguish
early trash from late trash provided a means by which to compare
the faunal remains that could be related to the first occupation of
Tijeras Pueblo to those representing the final occupation of the site
(see Young, this volume). The second goal was to determine if
there were differences in the ceramics from various areas of the
site that might indicate either spatially distinct activities, or
spatially separate social groups. Although southwestern archaeologists have addressed similar lines of inquiry for decades, their
resultant interpretations incorporate many untested assumptions.
Solutions to the problems of interpretation require research
beyond the scope of the analysis discussed here, but the technique
that is the focus of this chapter suggests one productive approach.

TRASH AS AN INFORMATION SOURCE

Most modern Americans consider trash the unwanted debris of
day-to-day living. Accumulations of garbage can become a cum-
bersome, unsightly burden that attract rodents and breeds disease.
These negative aspects of trash require our thought and attention.
Environmentally sensitive individuals and communities may re-
cycle trash through composting, landfill projects, the production
of alcohol, or the creation of art objects such as pop top sculpture.
In less affluent societies, material products are often reused or
recycled more extensively. Glass beverage bottles in Latin American towns, for example, are reused as storage containers. When
broken, the glass sherds may be set into the tops of garden walls to
discourage thieves. But no matter how much recycling takes place,
eventually objects are discarded. Households may therefore invest
in garbage disposals and trash compactors. Communities may set

aside land as a communal dump. Larger towns and cities have elaborate institutions for trash collection and disposal. In general, our contemporary solution to the problems associated with the accumulation of refuse is to set aside acceptable dumping areas where trash can be forgotten.

The broken or unwanted items that we consider trash provide a great deal of information for the archaeologist. Trash may sometimes be a more accurate reflection of behavior than what people say about themselves. For example, William Rathje of the University of Arizona compared data from interviews with Tucson residents and data from garbage collected in that city. He found that the "backdoor data" provide less biased information about household food discard behavior in the United States than can be obtained through interviews (Rathje 1978). The recovery of foetal animals from the trash at Tijeras Pueblo indicated that although modern Pueblo Indians express strong feelings against hunting in the early spring, their ancestors did some hunting year round (Young, this volume; see also Cordell 1977c).

Natural and cultural factors condition the manner in which trash is deposited and eventually recovered by the archaeologist. Heavy rains may wash materials downslope, rodents may mix and displace materials, and dogs may remove bones from trash deposits. Although from our perspective, trash comprises only unused or unwanted debris, other societies have different attitudes and behaviors about trash. Alfonso Ortiz explains that among some of the modern Rio Grande Pueblos, "All objects which have been used by people are endowed with sacredness because they are associated with the souls and with the sacred past" (Ortiz 1969: 20). Trash mounds that contain such objects are therefore somewhat sacred places, and among the Pueblos some shrines are located in refuse mounds. Probably, in part for similar reasons, burials were placed in trash mounds prehistorically.

In most prehistoric Pueblo sites, trash is found in special dumping areas. At Tijeras Pueblo, trash dumps were placed on the north and south sides of the main mound. Trash dumps were also situated on the south side of the early outlying roomblocks, and some abandoned rooms were filled with trash. The locations of trash areas suggest that each dump contained refuse from several households rather than from the dwellings immediately adjacent to the dump. One cannot, therefore, correlate the cessation of use of a trash area with the abandonment date of a particular series of rooms. Nevertheless, two factors enabled us to address the relative sequence of trash deposition at Tijeras Pueblo. First, in undisturbed trash mounds, the earlier material occurs in the lower levels and later material is most abundant in the upper levels (Figure 61). Second, in several instances, trash could be associated with the earlier occupation of the site, because late rooms had been built on top of these dumps and effectively sealed them off.

CERAMICS AND TIME AT TIJERAS PUEBLO

As Warren (this volume) indicates, ceramic types are used widely as the basis for dating sites in the Southwest. Ideally, changes in ceramic types reflect changes through time. Tijeras Pueblo is typical of many sites, however, in that the well-dated types present were manufactured and discarded throughout the occupation of the site. No new types were introduced while the site was inhabited nor did any of the earlier types disappear from the assemblage. The predominant, well-dated types are present throughout. Only their relative abundance varies slightly. In addition, as is common, the most frequent ceramic types recovered are nonpainted culinary wares that were used over very long periods of time and for that reason are not good temporal markers. In order to see if the ceramic types could be used to refine the

61. Stratified trash deposit at Tijeras Pueblo. In the layers of accumulated debris, the oldest material is on the bottom.

chronology of the site, we needed a technique that would allow us to distinguish those particular ceramic types that showed the most variation over time within the site.

In some studies, ceramic chronologies of single sites are based on the relative numbers of ceramic types found on abandoned room floors. The assumption basic to these chronological reconstructions is that the frequencies of types found on floors reflect the frequencies in which these types were being used when the room was abandoned. This assumption is questionable. If a room is abandoned while the site is still occupied, it is possible that the room may be completely cleared out. In this case, any ceramic fragments found on the floor would have been deposited somewhat later than the room ceased to be lived in. Second, if ceramic vessels, whole or broken, were left on room floors, the types represented might reflect the functions of the rooms rather than the times of their abandonment. Thus, one might expect a predominance of plain jars in a storage room no matter when that room was deserted.

In the excavation of Tijeras Pueblo, we found very few sherds on room floors, indicating that most ceramic items had been removed. Also, only a few of the earlier rooms were excavated, and the possibility of functional bias of these rooms could not be ignored. We did not feel confident that the relative numbers of different types of ceramics found on early or late room floors were necessarily representative of the relative popularity of the types actually in use when the rooms were abandoned. For these reasons, the analytic technique needed was one that could be applied directly to the ceramics recovered from the trash dumps.

Finally, we knew that the trash dumps had been sampled differentially. That is, only a small portion of some areas had been excavated while others had been nearly completely excavated. Thus 50 Santa Fe Black-on-white sherds from area A, which has been totally excavated, may not necessarily be a more significant number than 10 Santa Fe Black-on-white sherds from area B, of which only 10 percent of the trash has been excavated. A statistical technique was needed that would emphasize relatively minor changes in ceramic assemblages, and would not be affected by the different sample sizes being compared.

The statistic selected is called G-square. G-square is a modification of chi-square and was first used in archaeological research by Mark Harlan of the University of New Mexico, to study variation in anthropomorphic figurines at Chalcatzingo, Morales, Mexico (Harlan 1979). G-square is a distance statistic, measuring the similarity, or lack of it, between cases being compared. Analysis proceeds pairwise, making all possible nonredundant comparisons. If ten areas were samples, area 1 would be compared to areas 2 through 10, one at a time. Then area 2 would be compared to areas 3 through 10, one at a time, and so on until each area has been compared with every other area. G-square, unlike chi-square, is not influenced by sample size; therefore, it neither supresses nor exaggerates the effect of rare attributes, making it possible to monitor relatively minor variations in the ceramic assemblages. The presence of only two or three Chupadero sherds would not be swamped, and thus ignored, when compared with twenty Chupadero sherds from a sample five times larger.

THE USE OF CERAMIC TYPES AT TIJERAS PUEBLO

Many studies of social and/or temporal distance within a single site examine the distribution of design elements observed on ceramic sherds and not the distribution of types of ceramics (e.g. Longacre 1970). At Tijeras the design element approach was not feasible for two reasons. First, the size of the sherds at Tijeras is unusually small. Many fragments are no larger than a thumbnail. Some sherds of painted types show only the slip or background color. Most others have only a single line. These could not be used for a study of design elements. Second, painted decoration on the glaze types often consists of only one or two lines or bands below the rim of bowls. Thus, there is little variability in design elements. For the purposes of this study then, ceramic types based on technological attributes were used rather than design elements.

The use of ceramic types required that the types be identified with as much precision and consistency as possible. The ceramic fragments from Tijeras Pueblo were sorted by field school students according to traditional ceramic type descriptions. Accurate identification was difficult for a number of reasons. As mentioned, sherd size is unusually small. Also, three of the Black-on-white types, Galisteo Black-on-white, Santa Fe Black-on-white, and Wiyo Black-on-white, show considerable variation. Sherds of these types often exhibit attributes of more than one type, possibly because some were locally produced. For example, the Wiyo sherds are quite inconsistent in color, thickness, and in texture of paste. Many Wiyo sherds contain the light brown paste diagnostic of Wiyo but have the thick, crazed slip diagnostic of Galisteo Black- on-white. In order to check the accuracy of the identifications made by the field school students, a random sample of 1,153 sherds was taken. These sherds were sorted again and compared to the students' classification of them. The average error found was extremely low, less than 5 percent. Most of the error that did occur was in the identification of the Wiyo sherds. Because the margin of error in the field school counts was so low, and where the error might occur was known, the original counts of types made by the field school students were used in further analysis of the ceramics from the trash mounds.

G-SQUARE AND TEMPORAL CHANGE

The G-square technique was first used to determine which ceramic types were temporally sensitive. Sensitive types were searched for by determining which types were consistent and which were inconsistent in their abundance in the excavated levels of trash. The analysis compared type against type by level. For example, trash grid 020N 000W contained 15 levels, 2 A through 2 O. Fourteen ceramic types had been identified. These types included 10 painted types, plain ware, indented corrugated ware, smeared indented corrugated ware, and a miscellaneous category labeled other Black-on-white. A 14 by 15 matrix was created with the counts for ceramic types arranged in rows and excavation levels in columns (Figure 62).

The count for each type as it occurred throughout all levels was entered into a computer in this format. Thus, each of the fourteen types as they appeared throughout all levels were compared with each of the other types as they appeared throughout all of the levels. The comparison proceeded pairwise. A score was computed for statistical distance between types as they were compared. The higher the score, the greater the statistical distance between the types paired and therefore the greater variation in the relationship of paired types from level to level. The lower the score, the smaller the statistical distance between the paired types, indicating a relatively constant relationship. The ceramic types with consistently low scores, when compared with other types, oc-

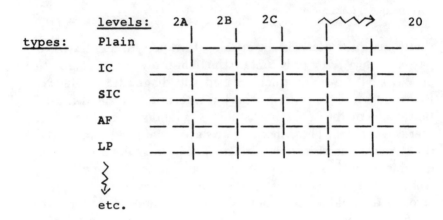

62. Matrix layout for G-Square analysis of ceramic types.

curred in about the same amounts through time. The ceramic types with consistently high scores when compared to other types varied from level to level. The high scoring types were variously being used in larger or smaller amounts than other types in use at the same time. They therefore represented the temporally sensitive types.

The temporally sensitive types were San Clemente Glaze Polychrome (SC), Santa Fe Black-on-white (SF), Los Padillas Glaze Polychrome (LP) and Heshotautla (Hesh). The other ceramic types did not contribute significantly to temporal variation and were eliminated from the next step in the analysis. This also made the matrices smaller.

The four selected ceramic types were then used in a search for significant temporal breaks in the levels of trash. This was done in order to determine which levels or grids of trash accumulated during the early occupation of the pueblo. For this purpose, ceramic counts of the selected types for each trash grid were organized into new matrices with the type counts in columns and the excavation levels in rows (Figure 63).

Using this format, the selected ceramic assemblage for each level may be compared with the ceramic assemblage of every other level pairwise. A low score indicates homogeneity or similarity. A high score indicates heterogeneity or dissimilarity. The point at which two adjacent levels have the highest score indicates where a temporal break probably occurs. This rough indication may be further refined by combining the ceramic counts by type

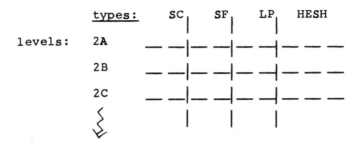

63. Matrix layout for G-Square analysis of stratigraphic levels.

for the levels above the suspected break, then comparing the two combined groups of levels. The suspected break may have to be adjusted up or down one or more levels to find the point at which a break actually occurs, if indeed one occurs at all. The ceramic assemblage representing the levels above the break will be homogeneous. The ceramic assemblage representing the levels below the temporal break will also be homogenous, but the two assemblages will be significantly different from one another. Each of the ten trash grids were searched in this manner for temporal breaks with the following results:

MAIN MOUND

GRID:		Temporal break occurred between levels:
000N	100E	2F/2G
000N	120E	2C/2D
000N	130E	NO BREAK, early trash, homogeneous throughout
020N	000W	possibly 2G/2H or 2I/2J (this grid is on a hillside and the remains were severely mixed)
000S	120E	C/D
100S	030E	E/F

OUTLIERS

GRID:		Temporal Break:
160N	030E	NO BREAK, EARLY
170N	130W	NO BREAK, EARLY
200N	370E	NO BREAK, EARLY
280N	320E	NO BREAK, EARLY

Because the application of the G-square technique is new, it was necessary to test the results against controlled situations. The tests were done by using the temporally sensitive types and computing G-square scores for trash areas that could be assigned to early or late occupations on the basis of other stratigraphic information. The cases included early occupation trash deposits that had been sealed by overlying late room floors. Another set of test cases was provided by the trash from the outlying roomblocks, which could be associated with the early occupation on the basis of tree-ring dates and the spatial configuration of the village. In all test cases, the breaks established on the basis of the G-square scores were confirmed. The accuracy of the method having been established, the temporal breaks that had been determined for the undated trash deposits were used to establish a temporal framework for the faunal remains (see Young, this volume)

G-SQUARE AND SPATIAL VARIATION

During the early occupation of Tijeras Pueblo, the site consisted of a series of separate roomblocks arranged in a rough circle (see Chapter 1). It is possible that each of these roomblocks might have been inhabited by socially separate groups, such as different extended families. It is also possible that the separate roomblocks might have been used primarily for community storage, another for ceremonial activities, and a third for ordinary habitation. If any of these possibilities occurred, we might expect heterogeneity in the ceramic assemblages from contemporary but spatially separate areas of the site, to reflect these behaviors. For example, if a small roomblock were the gathering place of a fraternal group that used only Los Padillas Glaze polychrome, the trash layers near that outlier might be dominated by Los Padillas sherds. In contemporary trash layers elsewhere in the Pueblo, the Los Padillas sherds would constitute a more moderate portion of the ceramic assemblage.

In order to examine the possibility that painted ceramic types, possibly representing different social groups, were differentially associated with early roomblocks, new G-square scores were computed. For this test, the matrix included all painted types rather than just those that were temporally sensitive. The statistic compared the abundance of each of the ten painted types pairwise, between each of the early roomblocks, including the early trash from the main mound. The G-square scores indicated homogeneity among the areas compared. The results do not preclude the possibility that different areas of the site were used or inhabited by different social groups. Rather, the results suggest that ceramic types may not be an appropriate measure of social group differentiation.

A final search of the ceramic assemblages from early occupation trash was made to determine if there were obvious differences in activities involving the use of ceramic vessels in different parts of the site. Ideally, the distribution of vessel forms, such as jars, ollas, and bowls, would have been the preferred index. It is generally assumed that these vessel forms are related to the function of the vessel. For example, open bowls are better suited to serving food than they are to storing water. Unfortunately, the small size of the sherds from Tijeras precluded determining vessel form with any confidence. Therefore, the amount of culinary ware (plain, corrugated, and indented corrugated) versus painted ware in the early trash on the main mound was compared to the amount of cooking ware versus plain ware in the trash from each of the early outlying roomblocks. Again, the G-square scores were very low, indicating homogeneity. Although this test was crude, because vessel form was not considered, the comparison indicated that the people in the outlying roomblocks were doing essentially the same things as those people living on the main mound. Everyone was breaking and discarding a good deal more of the plain cooking wares than the painted types.

In summary, we found that the application of an appropriate statistical technique was useful in providing a temporal framework for secondary trash deposits at Tijeras Pueblo. The statistical results were confirmed by independent stratigraphic data. The analysis indicates that standard ceramic types can be used for refined chronological control. The analyses did not allow us to differentiate spatially separate social groups or localized activity areas on the basis of variation in types among ceramic assemblages.

10

Interpretive Summary

Linda S. Cordell

Any report on completed excavation constitutes a temporary assessment of the past that is conditioned largely by the contemporary context within which archaeologists work. There are no definitive statements in the process of developing science. Science itself is an ever changing method of questioning. Each generation of archaeologists focuses on certain research questions as the result of academic training, experience, and interaction with colleagues. Research questions change as old issues are solved, or shelved, and as new areas of inquiry become apparent.

The research questions addressed here explicitly relate to describing the ways in which societies have adapted, over time, to an unpredictable and relatively nonproductive environment. This focus, as a research objective, was initially formulated by Judge (1974) and related to the excavation of Tijeras Pueblo. The primary concern was first to describe local prehistoric population changes, and second to determine the extent to which increases and decreases in population could be related to the availability of natural resources. The abundance of natural resources, such as food crops and game animals, might have changed through time because of shifts in rainfall or other climatic factors, or because of overexploitation by human beings. Although the Museum of New Mexico excavated sites because they were endangered by highway construction, the research orientation brought to both the collection and analysis of data recovered was essentially the same as that of the field school (Oakes 1978).

The information derived from excavation, site survey, historic documents, and interviews provides, in general terms, a reconstruction of the past population changes in the canyon. Rather meagre evidence suggests that the canyon was used only periodically or sporadically by Archaic hunters and gatherers. By about A.D. 700, long after domestic crops had been introduced into the Southwest, some agriculturalists were using Tijeras Canyon at least on a temporary basis. Between 900 and 1300, the number of sites in the canyon and the architecture of these sites, which suggests some permanence, indicate that an increase in population occurred, though it was not dramatic. The topographic settings selected for these sites, as well as the artifactual and botanical remains found in them, indicate that cultigens were economically important. Between about 1300 and 1425, relatively large sites were built in the canyon, but the overall population may not have greatly increased. Rather, there seems to have been aggregation of people at San Antonio and at Tijeras Pueblo. After 1425, the number of sites in the canyon declined and, presumably, the size of the resident population decreased. The canyon was used and inhabited into the historic period, as it is today, but from 1594 until the present, decreasing numbers of canyon residents derived their livelihood from the resources of the canyon.

The initial research design suggested that changes in resource use over time might be an indication of climate change (Judge 1974). We have found that the tree-ring studies provide the most direct index of rainfall fluctuations. Tree-ring data do not allow us to reconstruct the lengths of past growing seasons, the frequency of short growing seasons, or the seasonality of rainfall. We have not attempted to examine the periodicity of rainfall as reflected by the tree-rings. Nevertheless, the tree-ring studies show that rainfall was not strikingly different from modern conditions when the canyon was first inhabited by horticulturalists. The survey data for this time period, prior to 1300, indicate that the villages were very small and population density in the entire canyon was low. Given the current theoretical stance in archaeology to the effect that agriculture, which requires more labor investment than hunting and gathering, is the result of population pressure (Spooner 1972), we may ask why horticulture was practiced when population density was low.

Anderson and Oakes (this volume) suggest that agriculture may have been necessary to sustain the population over the winter. Horticulture would then have provided a storable buffering resource rather than a resource necessary to alleviate the stress of high populations. This notion is supported by the analysis of faunal remains (Young, this volume). Only at Coconito, the first year-round occupation of the canyon, was game hunted according to the cost effective, mini-max strategy. In other words, the frequency of game animals at Coconito suggests that hunting concentrated on the most abundant, locally available, and largest animals. This hunting strategy may only have been practical at this early period, when there was no competition among villages for game and when horticultural activities were not so time-consuming as to provide major scheduling conflicts with hunting. Unfortunately, we have no skeletal remains from this period, but we suggest that Coconito burials would not show the mortality patterns and dietary deficiencies evident at Tijeras Pueblo.

As noted, the tree-ring studies indicate the Tijeras Canyon was not a particularly favored environment for horticulture when it was first inhabited on a year-round basis. Why then was it inhabited by villagers at all? Two possible reasons are suggested by the ethnohistoric data and by the ceramic analyses in the context of current theory. The ethnohistoric data suggest the possibility that communities may have been established, as they were in Colonial times, to protect larger population aggregates in the Rio Grande Valley. However, neither the locations of the early farming villages, which were near alluvial lands, nor the configuration of these sites, an open pattern of small roomblocks, indicates that community defense was a major consideration. More important, there is no evidence of any group large enough to have been an effective threat.

Alternatively, it is possible that regional population densities were high enough so that some people were gradually forced to make a living in less than desirable settings. The petrographic analyses (Warren, this volume) indicate that the earliest ceramics in the canyon show links to the south and southwest. The area between Tijeras Canyon and Socorro, including the Albuquerque area, has not been systematically surveyed. The modern population density in Albuquerque itself, and along much of the central Rio Grande, precludes adequate assessment of the number of sites that may relate to this time period. As noted, however, the presence of earlier villages in the Albuquerque area (Frisbie 1967; Reinhart 1967) makes the notion of regional population pressure tenable. One need not assume either very large sites or densely packed communities. Rather, regional populations might be dense enough to effect movement into Tijeras Canyon simply because nearly all topographic settings that could support horticultural communities were in use.

The tree-ring data show that both the maximum population in the canyon, and the maximum clustering of population between 1300 and 1425, coincide with the period of greatest relative abundance of rainfall. Population aggregation in the canyon, at least, was not triggered by drought, although other climate-related stress has not been tested. Again, referring to the discussion by Anderson and Oakes (this volume), it appears that in the modern world among societies at low population densities where there is higher rainfall, dependence on agriculture increases while labor intensity does not. Tijeras does not, of course, provide an adequate test of this proposed relationship. However, the Tijeras data suggest lines of evidence that should be pursued further. First, the faunal studies (Young, this volume) indicate minor shifts in hunting strategies, meat processing, and cooking techniques that would not conflict with agricultural activities. Second, the skeletal remains show rather high incidences of iron deficiencies that may be related to increased consumption of corn and other plant foods. Third, it is possible that population aggregation itself is one consequence of an increased reliance on horticulture. The possible relationship between aggregation and horticulture is not suggested by current theory in anthropology. In fact, behavioral theory that purports to explain aggregation of human populations among nonmarket, nonindustrial societies is poorly developed. However, as noted in the Introduction, scheduling conflicts among horticulture, hunting and gathering, and other activities are minimized when the labor force necessary for these activities is readily available.

Village aggregation coincided with the first appearance of Rio Grande glaze ceramics, which are visually quite distinct from the black-on-white types predominant until then. In the past, archaeologists have sometimes argued that temporally coincident changes in ceramics and village plan indicate rapid cultural change brought about by the migration of ethnically distinct people into an area (Ford, Schroeder, and Peckham 1972). The changes in Tijeras do not appear to be the result of such migrations. First, the black-on-white ceramics seem to have been made (or at least discarded in high frequencies) throughout the period of Glaze A production. The change in ceramics is thus more apparent than real. Second, most of the early glazes were locally produced in the same manner as the black-on-white types. This suggests knowledge of local clay and temper sources as well as technological continuity. Finally, the types of trade ceramics that are present indicate ties with the south and west before the introduction of glaze. If any migration into the Tijeras area occurred, the people would seem to have come from the same localities as the original settlers.

The aggregation of people into villages as large as Tijeras Pueblo, initially perhaps two hundred people, requires social mechanisms to alleviate potential rivalries and conflicts among families. These need not have been elaborate, but they were surely important. The social mechanisms would have insured that enough people participated in planting and harvesting, in hunting and gathering, in manufacturing ceramics and other facilities and tools, and in participating in village maintenance. In societies where aggregated communities are particularly large or where communities participate in tightly integrated regional networks, hierarchies are quite formal and may be observed from archaeological data. In such societies, only a relatively few individuals have very high status. These persons will either live and/or be buried with more elaborate items than those without status. The papers by Young, Phillips, and Ferguson (this volume) suggest that social differentiation of this sort was not apparent in the Tijeras communities.

The tree-ring-derived rainfall patterns indicate that at the end of the 1300s and the beginning of the 1400s, optimal conditions were no longer present. The rainfall in the canyon again approximated modern conditions after rather more severe rainfall deficits than have been recorded recently in the area. The discussion by Anderson and Oakes (this volume) suggests that the change in climate should lead to increasing intensity of agriculture. The ethnohistoric studies (Quintana and Kayser, this volume) graphically illustrate how technologically difficult further agricultural intensification, sufficient to support further population growth or stabilize the economic base, would have been. The Hispanic water control technology involved using flumes and elaborate systems of ditches that have not been documented for prehistoric populations in the Rio Grande. More important, the Hispanic communities were not deriving their exclusive support from subsistence farming. The Hispanic settlers practiced a mixed economy of farming and herding and supplemented their incomes with timber cutting and mining. The social support of a nation-state or empire was not available to the Anasazi. For the Anasazi, the solution was decreasing the number of people relying on the canyon for their subsistence. Population decline is reflected first in the partial abandonment of Tijeras Pueblo and the building of a smaller village on the same site. Finally, San Antonio and Tijeras Pueblo were completely abandoned, although San Antonio was later reoccupied by a smaller number of people.

ANALYTIC PROBLEMS

All of the analyses presented here indicate the problems facing archaeological interpretation. These problems are not unique to our study; they are important issues in current archaeological writing (e.g., Schiffer 1976). The problems derive from the fact that the archaeological record is not a fossilized record of past behavior. Rather, items (even sites) are introduced into the archaeological record through processes that are only partially understood. In the context of the present discussion, for example, our analyses are hampered by a poor understanding of the cultural processes that lead to the introduction of plant materials into a room or trash deposit, the cultural factors in creating, maintaining, and abandoning trash middens, or the behavioral links between animals killed on the hunt and their bones recovered at sites. Once abandoned by the peoples who made and used them, archaeological materials are acted upon by natural, and frequently human, agents including archaeologists themselves. All of these actions disturb materials in as yet poorly defined ways. Thus, we do not know very much about the differential preserva-

tion of seeds or of animal bones of different densities in heterogeneous soil conditions, or the effect of rodent burrows in rooms
compared to their activities in trash deposits, or the loss to the
archaeological record of items robbed from sites by pot hunters, or
the total effect of disturbance created by careful and controlled excavation. Many of these and other problems are being addressed in
the continuing process of archaeological science, and refinement
in interpretation is to be an expected part of future research.

Each of our analyses was conditioned by behavioral models that
suggested areas of inquiry. Thus, Young's (this volume) economic
model of hunting was useful in order to specify deviations from
the expected patterns. The model of genetic distance (Ferguson,
this volume) and that of ceramic production (Warren, this volume)
were also useful in directing the focus of analyses and interpretation. But the models we work with today are, as we know, imper-
fect. They are based on current theories, some of which are better
developed than others, and all of which are subject to debate and
re-evaluation. Archaeologists should never be satisfied with the
models currently available. The process of science demands developing theory and models that allow more refined interpretation of
a wider variety of archaeological facts, as well as more comprehensive understanding of human behavior over time.

In addition to the analyses presented in this book, many other
analytic studies of the prehistory and history of Tijeras Canyon
are available, among them an analysis of the chipped stone projectile points from Tijeras Pueblo (Blevins 1974) and an analysis of
design symmetry of Tijeras ceramic vessels (Weisman 1977).
Other materials relating to the archaeology of Tijeras Canyon include field notes, summaries, photographs, and artifact catalogues
on file at the Laboratory of Anthropology, Museum of New Mexico, and at the Maxwell Museum of Anthropology at the University of New Mexico. All excavated material from Tijeras Pueblo is
available for future scholarly study at the Maxwell Museum.
Finally, a documentary film of the excavation of Tijeras Pueblo,
made cooperatively by the United States Forest Service, Southwestern Regional Office, and the University of New Mexico, is
available for and has been used for public education and Forest
Service training. All of these materials are being curated for the
future, because it is expected that research interests and research
methods will continue to change.

References

ABERT, J. W.
1962   *Abert's New Mexico Report 1846–1847* (Albuquerque: Horn and Wallace).
ADAMS, ELEANOR, AND FRAY ANGELICO CHAVEZ
1956   *The Missions of New Mexico, 1776*, (Albuquerque: University of New Mexico Press).
AEGERTER, E., AND J. A. KIRKPATRICK
1968   *Orthopaedic Diseases* (Philadelphia: W. B. Saunders).
ALLEN, J. W., AND C. H. McNUTT
1955   "A Pithouse Site Near Santa Ana Pueblo," *American Antiquity* 20(3):214–55.
ANDERSON, DANA
1977   Seminar Paper, Anthropology 454 (Manuscript on file, Department of Anthropology, University of New Mexico, Albuquerque).
ANGEL, J. L.
1969   "The Bases of Paleodemography," *American Journal of Physical Anthropology* 30:427–38.
BAILEY, HARRY P.
1960   "A Method of Determining the Warmth and Temperateness of Climate," *Geografiska Annaler* 42(1):1–16.
BAILEY, VERNON
1932   "Mammals of New Mexico," *North American Fauna* no. 53.
BANNISTER, BRYANT, JEFFREY S. DEAN, AND ELIZABETH A. M. GELL
1966   *Tree-Ring Dates from Arizona E*, Laboratory of Tree-Ring Research (Tucson: University of Arizona).
BANNISTER, BRYANT, JOHN W. HANNAH, AND WILLIAM J. ROBINSON
1966   *Tree-Ring Dates from Arizona K*, Laboratory of Tree-Ring Research (Tucson: University of Arizona).
BASS, WILLIAM
1971   *Human Osteology: A Lab and Field Manual* (Columbia: Missouri Archaeological Society).
BEAGLEHORN, ERNEST
1936   *Hopi Hunting and Hunting Ritual*, Yale University Publications in Anthropology, no. 4 (New Haven).
BINFORD, LEWIS R.
1968   "Post-Pleistocene Adaptations," in *New Perspectives in Archaeology*, ed. Sally R. Binford and Lewis R. Binford (Chicago: Aldine), pp. 313–42.
BINFORD, LEWIS R.
1980   "Willow Smoke and Dog's Tails: Hunter-Gatherer Settlement Systems and Archaeological Site Formation," *American Antiquity* 45(1):4–20.
BINFORD, LEWIS R., AND JACK B. BERTRAM
1977   "Bone Frequencies—and Attritional Processes," in *For Theory Building in Archeology*, ed. Lewis R. Binford (New York: Academic Press), pp. 77–153.
BLEVINS, BYRON B.
1974   "An Analysis of Qualitative Projectile Point Attributes with Regard to Resource Depletion," (Manuscript on file, Department of Anthropology, University of New Mexico, Albuquerque).

187

BLEVINS, BYRON B., AND CAROL JOINER
1977   "The Archeological Survey of Tijeras Canyon," *Archeological Report* no. 18 (Albuquerque: USDA Forest Service, Southwestern Region), pp. 126–52.

BOHRER, VORSILA L.
1970   "Ethnobotanical Aspects of Snaketown, A Hohokam Village in Southern Arizona," *American Antiquity* 35:4:413–30.

BOHRER, V. L., AND KAREN R. ADAMS
1977   *Ethnobotanical Techniques and Approaches at Salmon Ruin, New Mexico*, San Juan Valley Archaeological Project Technical Series no. 2, Contributions in Anthropology vol. 8, no. 1 (Portales: Eastern New Mexico University).

BOSERUP, ESTER
1965   *The Conditions of Agricultural Growth* (Chicago: Aldine).

BOWDEN, J. J.
1969   *Private Land Claims in the Southwest*, 6 volumes (Master of Law Thesis, Southern Methodist University, Dallas).

BRYAN, KIRK
1929   "Floodwater Farming," *Geographical Review* 19(3):444–46.

CARLSON, ROY L.
1961   "White Mountain Red Ware: A Stylistic Tradition in the Prehistoric Pottery of East Central Arizona," Anthropological Papers of the University of Arizona 19 (Tucson).

CASTETTER, EDWARD P.
1935   "Uncultivated Native Plants Used As Sources of Food," Volume 1 of *Ethnobiological Studies in the American Southwest*, University of New Mexico Bulletin 266, Biological Series vol. 4, no. 1 (Albuquerque).

CASTETTER, E. P. AND W. H. BELL
1942   *Pima and Papago Indian Agriculture* (Albuquerque: University of New Mexico Press).

CASTETTER, E. P., AND M. E. OPLER
1936   "The Ethnobiology of the Chiricahua and Mescalero Apache," *Ethnobiological Studies in the American Southwest*, University of New Mexico Bulletin 297, Biological Series vol. 4, no. 5 (Albuquerque).

CHANG, JEN-HU
1968   *Climate and Agriculture* (Chicago: Aldine).

CLARK, P. J.
1956   "The Heritability of Certain Anthropometric Characters Ascertained From Measurements of Twins," *American Journal of Human Genetics* 8:49–54.

CLARKE, S.
1977   "Mortality Trends in Prehistoric Populations," *Human Biology* 49:181–86.

COBB, SANDRA
1978   "Pottery Mound Analysis," (Unpublished Paper on file at University of New Mexico Osteology Lab, Albuquerque).

COHEN, MARC N.
1977   *The Food Crisis in Prehistory* (New Haven: Yale University Press).

COOK, EARL
1971   "The Flow of Energy in an Industrial Society," *Scientific American* 224(3): 134–44.

COOK, SARAH LOUISE
1930   "The Ethnobotany of Jemez Indians" (Master's thesis, University of New Mexico).

CORDELL, LINDA S.
1975   "The 1974 Excavation of Tijeras Pueblo, Cibola National Forest, New Mexico,"

Archeological Report no. 5 (Albuquerque: USDA Forest Service, Southwestern Region).

1977a   "The 1975 Excavation of Tijeras Pueblo, Cibola National Forest, New Mexico," *Archeological Report* no. 18 (Albuquerque: USDA Forest Service, Southwestern Region), pp. 1–43.

1977b   "The 1976 Excavation of Tijeras Pueblo, Cibola National Forest, New Mexico," *Archeological Report* no. 18 (Albuquerque: USDA Forest Service, Southwestern Region), pp. 169–200.

1977c   "Late Anasazi Farming and Hunting Strategies: One Example of a Problem in Congruence," *American Antiquity* 42(3):449–61.

CORDELL, LINDA S., AND FRED PLOG
1979   "Escaping the Confines of Normative Thought: A Reevaluation of Puebloan Prehistory," *American Antiquity* 44(3):405–29.

CULLY, ANN C.
1979   "Some Aspects of Pollen Analysis in Relation to Archaeology," *The Kiva* (44)23:95–100.

n.d.   "Plants Collected in the Vicinity of Tijeras Pueblo," (Manuscript on file, Department of Anthropology, University of New Mexico, Albuquerque).

DAVIS, JAMES T.
1960   "An Appraisal of Certain Speculations on Prehistoric Puebloan Subsistence," *Southwestern Journal of Anthropology* 16:15–21.

DITTERT, A. E., JR.
1959   "Culture Change in the Cebolleta Mesa Region, Central Western New Mexico," (Ph.D. Dissertation, University of Arizona, Tucson).

DOUGLASS, A. E.
1929   "The Secret of the Southwest Solved by Talkative Tree-Rings," *The National Geographic Magazine* 54(2):736–70.

EISELEY, LOREN
1957   *The Immense Journey* (New York: Vintage).

ELMORE, FRANCIS H.
1944   *Ethnobotany of the Navajo*, Monograph 392, series vol. 1, no. 7 (Albuquerque: University of New Mexico and the School of American Research).

EL-NAJJAR, M. Y., AND A. L. ROBERTSON, JR.
1976   "Spongy Bones in Prehistoric America," *Science* 193:141–43.

EL-NAJJAR, M. Y., D. J. RYAN, C. G. TURNER II, AND B. LOZOFF
1976   "The Etiology of Porotic Hyperostosis Among the Prehistoric and Historic Anasazi Indians of the Southwestern United States," *American Journal of Physical Anthropology* 44(3):447–88.

EULER, ROBERT C., GEORGE J. GUMERMAN, THORN N. V. KARLSTROM,
JEFFREY S. DEAN, AND RICHARD H. HEVLY
1979   "The Colorado Plateaus: Cultural Dynamics and Paleoenvironment," *Science* 205 (4411):1089–1101.

FARWELL, ROBIN E.
1977   "Report on Archaeological Excavations of Four Sites Along New Mexico State Highway I-40, Tijeras Canyon, New Mexico," (Manuscript on file, Laboratory of Anthropology, Museum of New Mexico, Santa Fe).

FINDLEY, JAMES S., ARTHUR H. HARRIS, DON E. WILSON, AND CLYDE JONES
1975   *Mammals of New Mexico* (Albuquerque: University of New Mexico Press).

FLANNERY, KENT V.
1972   "The Origins of the Village as a Settlement Type in Mesoamerica and the Near East: A Comparative Study," *Man, Settlement, and Urbanism*, ed. Peter J. Ucko,

Ruth Tringham, and G. W. Dimbleby (London: Gerald Duckworth and Co.), pp. 23–54.

FORDE, D. DARYLL
1931   "Hopi Agriculture and Land Ownership," *The Royal Anthropological Institute Journal* 61:357–405.

FRIEDLANDER, J. S.
1970   "Isolation by Distance on Bougainville Island," *American Journal of Physical Anthropology* 33:129–30.

FRISBIE, THEODORE R.
1967   "The Excavation and Interpretation of the Artificial Leg Basket Maker III–Pueblo I Sites Near Corrales, New Mexico" (Master's Thesis, Department of Anthropology, University of New Mexico, Albuquerque).

FRITTS, HAROLD C.
1976   *Tree Rings and Climate* (London: Academic Press).

GENOVES, SANTIAGO
1967   "Proportionality of Long Bones and Their Relation to Stature Among MesoAmericans," *American Journal of Physical Anthropology* 26:67–78.

GILLULY, JAMES, AARON WATERS, AND A. O. WOODFORD
1951   *Principles of Geology* (San Francisco: Freeman and Co.), 3rd ed.

GLADWIN, HAROLD S.
1945   "The Chaco Branch. Excavation at White Mound and in the Red Mesa Valley," *Medallion Papers* no. 38 (Globe, Arizona).

GLASSOW, MICHAEL A.
1972   "Changes in the Adaptations of Southwestern Basketmakers: A Systems Perspective," *Contemporary Archaeology: A Guide to Theory and Contributions* ed. Mark P. Leone (Carbondale: Southern Illinois University Press), pp. 289–302.

GUNNERSON, DOLORES A.
1974   *The Jicarilla Apaches: A Study in Survival* (DeKalb: University of Northern Illinois Press).

HACK, J. T.
1942   "The Changing Environment of the Hopi Indians of Arizona," *Papers of the Peabody Museum of American Archaeology and Ethnology* vol. 35, no. 1.

HANSON, N. R.
1958   *Patterns of Discovery* (Cambridge: Cambridge University Press).

HARLAN, MARK E.
1979   "An Inquiry into the Development of Complex Society at Chalcatzingo, Morelos, Mexico: Methods and Results," *American Antiquity* 44(3):471–93.

HARRIS, MARVIN
1971   *Culture, Man, and Nature: An Introduction to General Anthropology* (New York: Crowell).

HAURY, EMIL W.
1976   *The Hohokam Desert Farmers and Craftsmen, Excavations at Snaketown, 1964–1965* (Tucson: University of Arizona Press).

HIBBEN, FRANK C.
1941   "Evidences of Early Occupation in Sandia Cave, New Mexico and Other Sites in the Sandia–Manzano Region," *Smithsonian Miscellaneous Collections* 99(23): 1–44.

HOOTON, E. A.
1930   *The Indians of Pecos Pueblo* (New Haven: Yale University Press).

HOWELL, NANCY
1973   "The Feasibility of Demographic Studies in Anthropological Genetics," in *Methods and Theories of Anthropological Genetics*, ed. M. H. Crawford and P. L.

Workman (Albuquerque: University of New Mexico Press, School of American Research Advanced Seminar Series), pp. 249–62.

HOWELLS, W. W.

1953   "Correlations of Brothers in Factor Scores," *American Journal of Physical Anthropology* 11:121–29.

HRDLIČKA, A.

1908   "Physiological and Medical Observations Among the Indians of the Southwestern United States and Northern Mexico," *Bureau of American Ethnology Bulletin* 34 (Washington: Smithsonian Institution).

IRWIN-WILLIAMS, CYNTHIA

1967   "Picosa: The Elementary Southwestern Culture," *American Antiquity* 32(4): 441–56.

1973   *The Oshara Tradition: Origins of Anasazi Culture*, Eastern New Mexico University Contributions in Anthropology 5(1) (Portales).

JOCHIM, MICHAEL A.

1976   *Hunter-Gatherer Subsistence and Settlement a Predictive Model* (New York: Academic Press).

JORDE, LYNN B.

1977   "Precipitation Cycles and Cultural Buffering in the Prehistoric Southwest," in *For Theory Building in Archaeology*, ed. Lewis R. Binford (New York: Academic Press), pp. 385–96.

JUDGE, W. J.

1973   *The PaleoIndian Occupation of the Central Rio Grande Valley, New Mexico* (Albuquerque: University of New Mexico Press).

1974   "The Excavation of Tijeras Pueblo 1971–1973: Preliminary Report, Cibola National Forest, New Mexico," *Archeological Report* no. 3 (Albuquerque: USDA Forest Service, Southwestern Regional Office).

KEHOE, THOMAS F., AND ALICE B. KEHOE

1960   "Observations On the Butchering Techniques at a Prehistoric Bison Kill in Montana," *American Antiquity* 25(3):420–23.

KEMP, WILLIAM

1971   "The Flow of Energy in a Hunting Society," *Scientific American* 224(3):104–15.

KIDDER, A. V., AND A. O. SHEPARD

1936   *The Pottery of Pecos*, vol. 2 of Papers of Phillips Academy, no. 7 (New Haven).

KILLAM, WILLIAM R.

n.d.   "Prehistoric Agricultural Feasibility in the Tijeras Canyhon Region," (Manuscript on file at the Laboratory of Anthropology, Museum of New Mexico, Santa Fe).

KIRKBY, ANNE V. T.

1973   *The Use of Land and Water Resources in the Past and Present Valley of Oaxaca, Mexico*, Memoir of the Museum of Anthropology, University of Michigan, no. 5 (Ann Arbor).

KIRSCHMANN, JOHN D.

1975   *Nutrition Almanac* (New York: McGraw Hill).

KNIGHT, PAUL J.

1978   "The Role of Seed Morphology in Identification of Archaeological Remains," (Master's Thesis, University of New Mexico, Albuquerque).

KRAUSE, B. S., AND J. R. SCHWARTZMANN

1957   "Congenital Dislocation of the Hip in Fort Apache Indians," *Journal of Bone and Joint Surgery* 39A:448–49.

KUNITZ, S. J., AND R. C. EULER

1972   "Aspects of Southwestern Paleoepidemiology," *Anthropology Report* no. 2 (Prescott, Arizona: Prescott College Press).

LAMBERT, M. F.
1954   *Paa-Ko, Archaeological Chronicle of an Indian Village in North Central New Mexico*, parts I-V, Monograph 19 (Santa Fe: School of American Research).

LANGE, CHARLES H.
1959   *Cochiti: A New Mexico Pueblo, Past and Present* (Austin: University of Texas Press).

LAYRISSE, MIGUEL
1969   "Iron Absorption from Food," *Iron Metabolism and Anemia*, Pan American Health Organization Scientific Report 184, pp. 38–42.

LEE, RICHARD B.
1969   "!Kung Bushman Subsistence: An Input-Output Analysis," in *Environment and Cultural Behavior*, ed. Andrew P. Vayda (New York: Natural History Press), pp. 47–79.

LEE, RICHARD, AND IRVEN DEVORE
1966   *Man the Hunter* (Chicago: Aldine).

LIGON, J. STOKLEY
1961   *New Mexico Birds and Where to Find them* (Albuquerque: University of New Mexico Press, in cooperation with the New Mexico Department of Game and Fish).

LINSKY, PATRICIA K.
1974   "Cochise and Mogollon Hunting Patterns in West-Central New Mexico," in *Collected Papers in Honor of Florence Hawley Ellis*, ed. Theodore Frisbie. Papers of the Archaeological Society of New Mexico 2, pp. 246–71 (Albuquerque).

LONGACRE, WILLIAM A.
1966   "Changing Patterns of Social Integrations: A Prehistoric Example from the American Southwest," *American Anthropologist* 58(1):94–102.

1970   *Archaeology as Anthropology: A Case Study*, Anthropological Papers of the University of Arizona, no. 17 (Tucson).

1976   "Population Dynamics at Grasshopper Pueblo, Arizona," in *Demographic Anthropology*, ed. E. B. W. Zubrow (Albuquerque: University of New Mexico Press, School of American Research Advanced Seminar Series), pp. 169–84.

LUMPKIN, CHARLES
1976   "A Multivariate Craniometric Analysis of Selected Southwestern Archeological Populations" (Ph.D. dissertation, University of New Mexico, Albuquerque).

MacNEISH, RICHARD S.
1971   "Speculation About How and Why Food Production and Village Life Developed in the Tehuacan Valley, Mexico," *Archaeology* 24(4):307–15.

MARTIN, PAUL S., AND FRED T. PLOG
1973   *The Archaeology of Arizona* (Garden City, N.Y.: Doubleday Natural History Press).

MARTIN, WILLIAM C., AND CHARLES R. HUTCHINS
1975   *A Manual of the Flora of the Sandia Mountains, New Mexico* (Department of Biology, University of New Mexico, Albuquerque).

MATSON, F. R.
1960   "The Quantitative Study of Ceramic Materials," in *The Application of Quantitative Methods in Archaeology*, ed. R. F. Heizer and S. F. Cook, Viking Fund Publications in Anthropology, no. 28 (New York: Wenner-Gren Foundation).

MERA, H. P.
1933   *A Proposed Revision of the Rio Grande Glaze Paint Sequence*, Laboratory of Anthropology Technical Series no. 5 (Santa Fe).

1935   *Ceramic Clues to the Prehistory of North Central New Mexico*, Laboratory of Anthropology Technical Series Bulletin no. 8 (Santa Fe).

1940   *Population Changes in the Rio Grande Glaze-Paint Area*, Laboratory of Anthropology Technical Series Bulletin no. 9 (Santa Fe).

MIDDLE RIO GRANDE COUNCIL OF GOVERNMENTS

1974   *Decision-Making Guide for Land Use Planning 1, Soils Data Handbook* (Albuquerque).

MILES, J. S.

1975   *Orthopaedic Problems of Wetherill Mesa Populations*, National Park Service Publications in Archeology, 7G.

MINNIS, PAUL E., AND STEVEN A. LeBLANC

1976   "An Efficient, Inexpensive Arid Lands Flotation System," *American Antiquity* 41(4):491–93.

MURDOCK, GEORGE

1967   *Ethnographic Atlas* (Pittsburgh: University of Pittsburgh Press).

NAYLOR, JAMES N.

1964   "Plant Distribution of the Sandia Mountains Area, New Mexico," (Master's Thesis, Department of Biology, University of New Mexico, Albuquerque).

NELSON, N. C.

1916   "Chronology of the Tano Ruins, New Mexico," *American Anthropologist* 18(2):159–80.

NELSON, WENDY

1978   "Faunal Analysis of Tijeras Pueblo Rooms," (Manuscript on file, Department of Anthropology, University of New Mexico, Albuquerque).

NMSRC (NEW MEXICO STATE RECORDS CENTER, ARCHIVES DIVISION)

NMLG-SG (*New Mexico Land Grants, Surveyor General*) numbered cases on microfilm

SANM (*Spanish Archives of New Mexico*)

    I. Land and Property Archives

    II. Civil and Military Archives

OAKES, YVONNE

1978   "Excavations at Dead-Man's Curve, Tijeras Canyon, New Mexico: New Mexico State Highway Department Project I-040-3(55) 171 and I-040-3(36) 169," (Manuscript on file, Laboratory of Anthropology, Museum of New Mexico, Santa Fe).

ORTIZ, ALFONSO A.

1969   *The Tewa World* (Chicago: University of Chicago Press).

PUBLIC HEALTH SERVICE

1975   *United States Vital Statistics*; Health, Education, and Welfare.

RABIN, L., ET AL.

1965   "Untreated Congenital Hip Disease: A Study of the Epidemiology, Natural History, and Social Aspects of the Disease in a Navajo Population," *American Journal of Public Health* 55(2):1–44.

RAPPAPORT, ROY A.

1971   "The Flow of Energy in an Agricultural Society," *Scientific American* 224(3):116–32.

RATHJE, WILLIAM

1978   "Le Project du Garbage 1975: Historic Trade-Offs," in *Social Archeology*, ed. Charles L. Redman, Mary Jane Berman, Edward V. Curtin, William T. Langhorne, Jr., Nina M. Versaggi, and Jeffrey C. Wanser (New York: Academic Press), pp. 373–80.

REED, CHARLES A., EDITOR

1977   *Origins of Agriculture* (The Hague: Mouton Publishers).

REED, ERIK K.

1944   "The Abandonment of the San Juan Region," *El Palacio* 51.

1949   "Sources of Upper Rio Grande Culture and Population," *El Palacio* 56:163–84.

1958   "Comment," in *Migrations in New World Culture History*, ed. R. H. Thompson, *University of Arizona Social Science Bulletin* 27, (Tucson), pp. 7–8.

REINHART, THEODORE R.

1967   "The Alameda Phase: An Early Basketmaker III Culture in the Middle Rio Grande Valley, New Mexico," *Southwestern Lore* 33(1):24–32.

ROBBINS, WILFRED WILLIAM, JOHN PEABODY HARRINGTON, AND
BARBARA FREIRE-MARRECO

1916   "Ethnobotany of the Tewa Indians," *Bureau of American Ethnology* Bulletin 55 (Washington: Smithsonian Institution).

ROBINSON, WILLIAM

1977   "Preliminary Report on Tree-Ring Based Climate Reconstruction For Tijeras, New Mexico," (Manuscript on File, Department of Anthropology, University of New Mexico, Albuquerque).

SANDERS, WILLIAM T.

1968   "Hydraulic Agriculture, Economic Symbiosis and the Evolution of States in Central Mexico," in *Anthropological Archeology in the Americas* ed. Betty J. Meggers (Washington, D.C.: Anthropological Society of Washington).

SANDERS, WILHAIM, AND DAVID WEBSTER

1978   "Unilinealism, Multilinealism, and the Evolution of Complex Societies," in *Social Archaeology*, ed. Charles Redman et al. (New York: Academic Press).

SCHIFFER, MICHAEL B.

1976   *Behavioral Archaeology* (New York: Academic Press).

SCHORSCH, RUSSELL L.

1962   "A Basket Maker III Pit House Near Albuquerque," *El Palacio* 69(2):114–18.

SCHOEWETTER, JAMES, AND ALFRED E. DITTERT, JR.

1968   "An Ecological Interpretation of Anasazi Settlement Patterns," in *Anthropological Archaeology in the Americas* ed. Betty J. Meggers (Washington, D.C.: Anthropological Society of Washington).

SHEPARD, A. O.

1936   "The Technology of La Plata Pottery," in *The Pottery of Pecos* by A. D. Kidder and A. O. Shepard. Papers of the Phillips Academy vol. 2, no. 7 (New Haven).

1939   "The Technology of La Plata Pottery," in *Archaeological Studies in the La Plata District*, by E. H. Morris (Washington: Carnegie Institution)

1942   "Rio Grande Glaze-Paint Ware," *Contributions to American Anthropology and History* no. 39, Publication 528 (Washington: Carnegie Institution), pp. 129–262.

1953   "Notes on Color and Past Composition," in *Archaeological Studies in the Petrified Forest National Monument, Arizona*, by Fred Wendorf. Museum of Northern Arizona Bulletin 27, pp. 177–93 (Flagstaff).

1950   "Cited in D. O'Bryan, "Excavations in Mesa Verde National Park, 1947–48," *Medallion Paper* no. 39 (Globe, Arizona: Gila Pueblo).

1963   *Ceramics for the Archaeologist*, Publication 609 (Washington: Carnegie Institution).

SIMMONS, MARC

1969   "Settlement Patterns and Village Plans in Colonial New Mexico," *Journal of the West* 8(1):7–21.

SKINNER, S. ALAN

1965   "The Sedillo Site: A Pit House Village in Albuquerque," *El Palacio* 72(1):5–24.

SNOW, DAVID H.

1972   "Archeological Survey, New Mexico State Highway Project, Tijeras Canyon, I-40-3(18)69," (Manuscript on file, Laboratory of Anthropology, Museum of New Mexico, Santa Fe).

1976   "Cultural Resources Investigation and Recommended Program for Alleviation of

Direct and Indirect Impact on Archeological Sites in Cibola National Forest, New Mexico. New Mexico State Highway Department Project I-040-3(55) 171, Tijeras Canyon, New Mexico" (Manuscript on file, Laboratory of Anthropology, Museum of New Mexico, Santa Fe).

SOKAL, ROBERT R., AND F. JAMES ROHLF
1969   *Biometry* (San Francisco: W. H. Freeman and Co.).

SPOONER, BRIAN, EDITOR
1972   *Population Growth: Anthropological Implications* (Cambridge, Mass.: M.I.T. Press).

STANISLAWSKI, M. B.
1975   " 'What You See is What You Get': Ethnoarchaeology and Scientific Model Building," paper presented at the Fortieth Annual Meeting of the Society for American Archaeology, Dallas.

STEINBOCK, R. TED
1976   *Paleopathological Diagnosis and Interpretation* (Springfield, Illinois: Charles C. Thomas).

STEVENSON, MATILDA COXE
1915   *Ethnobotany of the Zuni*, Bureau of American Ethnology Thirtieth Annual Report (Washington: Smithsonian Institution).

STEWART, T. DALE
1957   "Distortion of the Pubic Symphyseal Surface in Females and Its Effect on Age Determination," *American Journal of Physical Anthropology* 15:9–18.

STOLTMAN, JAMES B.
1966   "New Radiocarbon Dates for Southeastern Fiber-Tempered Pottery," *American Antiquity* 3(6):872–74.

STRUEVER, M. B.
1977   "Relation of Pollen and Flotation Analyses to Archaeological Excavations, Chaco Canyon" (Master's Thesis, University of New Mexico, Albuquerque).

SWADESH, FRANCES LEON
1974   *Los Primeros Pobladores: Hispanic Americans of the Ute Frontier* (Notre Dame, Indiana: University of Notre Dame Press).
1976   "Archeology, Ethnohistory and the First Plaza of Carnuel," *Ethnohistory* 23(1):31–44.

SWADESH, FRANCES LEON
1977   "San Antonio: A Tijeras Canyon Village," An Ethnohistorical Report prepared for MNH Highway Project No. 63.05. (Manuscript on file, Laboratory of Anthropology, Museum of New Mexico, Santa Fe).

SWANK, GEORGE R.
1932   "The Ethnobotany of the Acoma and Laguna Indians," (Master's Thesis, University of New Mexico, Albuquerque).

SWITZER, RONALD R.
1969   *Tobacco, Pipes and Cigarettes of the Prehistoric Southwest*, Special Report no. 8 (El Paso, Texas: El Paso Archaeological Society).

TEGLIA, DEBORAH
1977   "Report on the Coconito Faunal Remains" (Manuscript on file, Laboratory of Anthropology, Museum of New Mexico, Santa Fe).

TIERNEY, GAIL D.
1976   *A Botanical Survey at Site LA 24, San Antonio, New Mexico*. Laboratory of Anthropology Notes no. 130 (Santa Fe).

TITIEV, M.
1944   *Old Oraibi: A Study of the Hopi Indians of Third Mesa*, Papers of the Peabody Museum of American Archaeology and Ethnology, vol. 22, no. 1 (Cambridge, Mass.: Harvard University).

TOULMIN, STEPHEN
1953   *The Philosophy of Science.* (London: Hutchinson University Library).
TUAN, YI-FU, CYRIL E. EVERARD, J. WIDDISON, AND I. BENNETT
1973   *The Climate of New Mexico* (Santa Fe: State Planning Office).
UBELAKER, DOUGLAS
1974   *Reconstruction of Demographic Profiles from Ossuary Skeletal Samples: A Case Study from the Tidewater Potomac,* Smithsonian Contributions in Anthropology, no. 18 (Washington).
U.S. DEPARTMENT OF AGRICULTURE
1937   *Tijeras Canyon–Moriarty Area Conservation Economics Series Regional Bulletin no. 12,* Soil Conservation Service, Region 8 (Albuquerque).
U.S. DEPARTMENT OF COMMERCE
1974   "Local Climatological Data," *Annual Summary with Comparative Data* (Albuquerque).
VEHIK, SUSAN C.
1978   "Bone Fragments and Bone Grease Manufacturing: A Review of Their Archeological Use and Potential,"Plains Anthropologist 22(7):169–82.
VIVIAN, R. GWINN
1974   "Conservation and Diversion: Water Control Systems in the Anasazi Southwest," in *Irrigations's Impact on Society,* ed. Theodore E. Downing and McGuire Gibson, University of Arizona Anthropological Papers 25 (Tucson), pp. 95–112.
VIVIAN, R. GWINN, AND NANCY WILKINSON CLENDENEN
1965   "The Denison Site: Four Pit Houses Near Isleta, New Mexico," *El Palacio* 72(2): 5–26.
VYTLACIL, NATALIE, AND J. J. BRODY
1958   "Two Pit Houses Near Zia Pueblo," *El Palacio* 65(5):174–84.
WALKER, J. M.
1977   "Congenital Hip Disease in a Cree-Ojibwa Population: A Retrospective Study," *Canadian Medical Association Journal* 116:501–4.
WARREN, A. H.
1968   "Petrographic Notes on Glaze Paint Pottery, in *The Cochiti Dam Archeology Salvage Project,* part I, Report on the 1963 Salvage Project, assembled by Charles H. Lange, Museum of New Mexico Research Records no. 6 (Santa Fe).
1969   "Tonque—One Pueblo's Glaze Pottery Industry," *El Palacio* 76(2):36–42.
1975   "An Archaeological Survey of the Proposed Mining Project Area," Occidental Mineral Corp., Cerrillos District, New Mexico (Santa Fe: Romco.).
1976   "The Geology and Mineral Resources of Carnuel," A Preliminary Report Prepared for the Laboratory of Anthropology, Museum of New Mexico, Santa Fe.
1977   "New Dimensions in the Study of Prehistoric Pottery," Appendix I in *Archaeological Investigations in the Cochiti Reservoir, New Mexico* ed. R. C. Chapman and Jan V. Biella. (Albuquerque: University of New Mexico)
WEATHERWAX, P.
1954   *Indian Corn in Old America* New York: Macmillan Co.).
WEISMAN, ELAINE
1977   "Symmetry Analysis of Rio Grande Glaze Pots" (Manuscript on file, Department of Anthropology, University of New Mexico, Albuquerque).
WEISS, K. M.
1976   "Demographic Theory and Anthropological Inference," *Annual Review of Anthropology* 5:351–81.
WENDORF, FRED
1953   *Archaeological Studies in the Petrified Forest National Monument,* Museum of Northern Arizona Bulletin 27 (Flagstaff).

WENDORF, FRED, AND ERIK K. REED
1955   "An Alternative Reconstruction of Northern Rio Grande Prehistory," *El Palacio* 62(5–6):131–73.

WHITE, L. A.
1962   "The Pueblo of Sia, New Mexico," Bureau of American Ethnology Bulletin 184 (Washington: Smithsonian Institution).

WHITE, THEODORE
1954   "Observations on the Butchering Techniques of Some Aboriginal Peoples: nos. 3, 4, 5," *American Antiquity* 19(2):160–64.

WHITING, A. F.
1939   *Ethnobotany of the Hopi*, Arizona Society of Science and Art Bulletin 15 (Flagstaff).

WILLEY, GORDON R., AND JEREMY A. SABLOFF
1980   *A History of American Archaeology*, 2nd ed. (San Francisco: W. H. Freeman and Co.).

WITTFOGEL, K., AND E. GOLDFRANK
1943   "Some Aspects of Pueblo Mythology and Society," *Journal of American Folklore* 56:17–30.

WOODBURY, RICHARD B.
1961   "Prehistoric Agriculture at Point of Pines, Arizona," *Society for American Archaeology Memoirs* 17.

YELLEN, JOHN E.
1977   "Cultural Patterning in Faunal Remains: Evidence from the Kung Bushmen," in *Experimental Archeology* ed. Daniel Ingersoll, John E. Yellen, and William Macdonald. (New York: Columbia University Press).

YOUNG, GWEN JARAHIAN
1978   "Analysis of the Faunal Remains of San Antonio" (Manuscript on file at the Laboratory of Anthropology, Museum of New Mexico, Santa Fe).

Index